Secret Guilt

By

Brenda Barnes

COLEMAN JONES
PRESS

Scriptures marked NIV are taken from the NEW INTERNATIONAL VERSION
(NIV): Scripture taken from THE HOLY BIBLE, NEW INTERNATIONAL
VERSION °. Copyright© 1973, 1978, 1984, 2011 by Biblica, Inc.™. Used by
permission of Zondervan. All rights reserved.

Scriptures marked NKJV are taken from the NEW KING JAMES VERSION
(NKJV): Scripture taken from the NEW KING JAMES VERSION°. Copyright©
1982 by Thomas Nelson, Inc. Used by permission. All rights reserved.

Published in Dallas, TX by Coleman Jones Press

www.ColemanJonesPress.com

ISBN: 978-1088011430

Praise for Secret Guilt

Brenda's story of how secret guilt can impact your life and how to take the steps to get rid of it, is spot on! You can't help but to take inventory of yourself and start praying over things that you didn't even realize were there. Truly a powerful story that anyone can relate to no matter what the source of their guilt is. In this case it was an abortion, but it's a story that's relevant to everyone, regardless of whether it's abortion-related or not. If you're dealing with guilt and shame or know someone who is, this is a must read! Truly healing!

Tracee Jones, Publisher | Author of Keeping the Vow: 21 Tips to Handling Dating, Attraction & Temptation for Christian Singles Practicing Purity

Glory to God! A book that all women can relate to. Raw and full of wisdom and lessons. Brenda is so brave and such a humble servant of the Lord. I would personally gift this to my daughter when she reaches her 18th birthday.

Deanne Monderin, Head of the Christian Education Department | Jesus Christ the Savior Fellowship, Author of Goodnight My Child

Through the author's transparency in this book, hurting women will be healed of their pain, and set free of their shame and defeat. Chains will be broken, and when you're done reading this book, you will be able to sing "I am free, praise the Lord, I'm free. No more chains are holding me." She has truly released the passion from her heart to the pages of this great book. Rufus and I are so very proud of you. Congratulations Brenda on your well-deserved success and great accomplishment.

Susie Smith

Her translucent story helps you find clarity and recognize guilt. This book encourages you to seek healing for not only yourself, but for all you come in contact with that are bound by guilt. Really incredible book!

Stefanie Potts, Founder of Purposely Parenting 365 |
Author of On My Way

In spite of dealing with her own feelings of guilt, shame, pain of disappointment, and even the abuse she encountered, still Brenda was able to speak healing into my life and the lives of so so many others. I am so thankful for her transparency as she shared her testimony with the world! It is clear that the Lord has been with her, strengthened her and made her more powerful! You'll be blessed by reading this book.

Linda Franklin

She never ceases to amaze me! To see her heart for helping others and her vulnerability by writing this book is nothing short of amazing. I know that many people will experience freedom and they will be touched by the anointing that's on Brenda Barnes' life, and in this book! Her words of encouragement have always lifted me out of my darkest days and now she's spreading that love and knowledge to all that read this book. I'm incredibly excited for what's to come.

Napolian Barnes, Jr., Executive Pastor

I am honored that I was one of the first to know your truth. You gave me strength in the face of defeat. I appreciated your candor that day sitting in Wendy's when I felt like I had the weight of the world on my shoulders. Now you're extending that same grace to others through this book. How awesome is that? You helped me become all I am today, and I'm eternally grateful. I want you to know that I am extremely proud of you for all of your accomplishments. You have worn so many roles over the years as a crown on your head, and quite gracefully might I add. From Wife, mother, grandmother, First Lady, business owner, motivational speaker, charity worker, cheerleader, friend, sister, and now Author! Ayana and I thank you and love you very much. Best wishes on this new endeavor!

Precious Abbott, N.P.

It's wonderful to see how Brenda's love for people has grown into a great passion for hurting women everywhere, and how she has truly allowed her light to shine. As her sister, I can tell you that she's a compassionate, caring, sharing, loving and giving person, who's not only God fearing and a powerful prayer warrior, but a beautiful person inside and out who will give you the shirt off her back. I could go on and on about what a beautiful person she is, and what a blessing she has been to me as a sister. Congratulations on your book, Brenda! May God bless this book, and may it bless many! So proud to say "you're my sister!"

Artelia Smith

To my wife Brenda, it gives me great pleasure to know you have successfully finished writing your first book. I don't have words to tell you how happy and proud I am of you. Congratulations baby and best wishes to you on your accomplishments. I always knew that you were capable of doing something great like this. Your success is really proof of your hard work, dedication, and sacrifice. I was there seeing you waking up at 3am in the morning writing; with that being said this is surely a moment of great celebration for me as well as our children and grandchildren. I am confident that this book will touch many women as well as men. Congratulations!

Your husband, Napolian Barnes

Acknowledgements

I want to thank God first, for making this possible.

I want to also thank God for my awesome husband Napolian Sr. who had to listen to my storylines at late hours. Thanks, hunny. Love You!

Thanks to my son Napolian Jr. for constantly reassuring me and encouraging me to complete this assignment and giving me so much helpful guidance and support. Love you, Son!

I want to thank my baby girl, Precious, for calling and making sure that I stayed focused, and listening to me from day to day as I shared my story, and for encouraging me to stay at it. Baby girl, I love you!

Special thanks to Krista Smith and La'Boris Cole, for the great insights you shared in my book, and the love and support and sharing great input!! I greatly appreciate you both.

I want to thank God for my supportive sisters, Susie, Artelia, Sheila, and my twin sister Linda, who pushed and encouraged me daily, and for my brother-in-laws Rufus and Roy, and all of my supportive nieces, nephews, and cousins. Love You!

Thank God for Tracee and Ross Jones, my Publishers at Coleman Jones Press, and their team. I couldn't have done this without you accepting to publish my book. You listened and heard my passion and you helped make this happen. Thank you, Ross for your constant encouragement, coaching, and push for me do my videos when I didn't believe I could do them. Thanks to you both.

Thanks to my cousin, Dewonna, for introducing me to Tracee and encouraging me to go forward with writing my book.

Thanks to my friends Gayle Tullis, Jeretta Saunders, Jackie Mills, Rolonda Griggs, and Lehester Thorton who always found words of encouragement during this process, and for all your support.

Table of Contents

Foreword

Today's culture presses us to often suppress things and save face to keep our name intact. How many people have been taught to just keep quiet, move on, and everything will be ok? It is appalling to consider how many spiritual leaders have spoken messages with this tone and have (in some kind of way) contributed to people staying bound to their past mistakes and experiences that had nothing to do with them.

Brenda Barnes has decided to challenge the culture of "Shut up and move on" and is speaking out about her life experiences in attempt to encourage, inspire and empower others to be free like her. This book is going to challenge you to look into the mirror and really get real with yourself. Secret Guilt will have you asking yourself the million-dollar question: Have I been honest with myself? Have I suppressed something that has impacted my relationships, marriage, my relational capacity or just my perspective on life?

Secret Guilt was birthed out of pain, tears, and the Holy Spirit to bring freedom and hope to those who have been imprisoned by their past and it will give the readers a guide to wholeness. It's no longer good enough to read good books, hear great sermons and not walk away with practical steps to better your life.

As her son, I am so proud of her courage to face her guilt head on. She has inspired me to be a better leader and man by being vulnerable and transparent with others in order to lead them to their promise land. I pray that everyone who reads this book will feel the power of God's love and will share this book with others because if we all are honest, we all have SECRET GUILT!

Napolian Barnes, Jr.
Executive & Worship Pastor
Word of Truth Family Church - Arlington, TX

CHAPTER ONE

Taking it to the Grave

There are some secrets that are safe to share. Then there are those secrets that you just know deep inside your soul, that you'd better keep to yourself and take to the grave, because if anyone knew what you did, or what happened to you, it would bring a fate worse than death. I'm sure you know what I'm talking about. There are those secrets we keep that are not really that embarrassing or life-threatening. These are the type of things that you prefer that people didn't know about you, so you just don't share that side of yourself with anyone. This type of secret is one that you simply hope certain people never find out about you. It's not the type of secret that would ruin your life if it just so happened to get out.

Then there are those secrets, the things you've done, that you know if anyone knew about you, would simply ruin everything, and bring about shame, humiliation, and possibly separation from the people you love and anything good in your life. This is the type of secret that if revealed could cause public disgrace if you're in a high-profile role --- whether that's in your career, in ministry, on social media, whatever. When you're carrying this type of secret, sometimes it's just better (and far safer) to keep your secret to yourself and take it with you to the grave.

Well, at least that's what I believed, and it's how I lived for 31 years of my life --- having no idea that my secret (though as hidden and buried as it was) had taken root, developed a voice, and was wreaking havoc on my life in ways that I didn't think possible, until the day came when I realized I would have to face my worst nightmare, and deal with it.

I remember it like it was yesterday. I was 19 years old with a bright future and my whole life ahead of me. I had just started college, and was finding my place in the world, when I met a guy who was interested in me. He was ten years older than me, but we had some things in common, and there was something about him that felt both exciting and safe. At that time, I was new to the world of dating. In fact, you could say I was very naïve. I was this church girl who grew up in a super sanctified home, and my mom, Lucille Ruff, kept us in church. But she didn't just keep us in church, she kept us on our knees as well --- me, my sisters, and my cousins. To say that she believed in prayer was an understatement.

My mom would pray so long until it would get just downright annoying to me, so I would make these sounds. I'd breathe hard, sigh, and do anything to get my point across that she was praying too long. We would fall asleep while she was praying, wake up, and she would still be praying. Finally, I would muster up enough courage and say "Mom, you not through yet? It doesn't take all of this!" Then I'd feel the switch (if you don't know what a switch is, it's a thin tree branch that's about as wide as one of your fingers) that she kept on the side of her bed, pop across my back, and she'd reply "It takes all of this and then some!" Then she'd remind me "and you're going to need it the most." Somehow, she just knew things.

Growing up in a religious home with a Holiness background, boys and dating was not something that my sisters and I were allowed to do, so when I became grown (or so I thought) and started dating this guy, I wasn't really open to my mom's opinion of him. The first time she saw him, she said, "Brenda, he's not the one." But me, being the *Ms. Know it All* that I was, ignored her altogether. I was always kind of strong-willed and had a mind of my own, which one day – about six months later, to be exact -- would cost me a great deal of pain and regret.

One day after my boyfriend and I had gone out, he brought me back to his house. On this particular day, he was acting strange and was very moody. It seemed like everything I did, bothered him. I should've known that something was wrong, and should've left, but I didn't. I stayed thinking we would talk about it.

We were sitting in his living room, and he was playing music rather loudly, and drinking. I crossed over him to turn down the music, and the next thing I felt was this pain from where he had hit me, and knocked me to the floor, and began to sexually assault me. I pleaded with him to stop, but he kept saying to me over and over again, "Look, what you made me do. I can't help myself. You're just so beautiful. You're just so beautiful."

If you've ever had this happen to you, then you know it's a horrific experience, and one that is difficult to forget. I blamed myself for the events that occurred, believing that somehow, I had brought it on myself, and that this was my fault. Back then, when something like this happened, it wasn't called date-rape like it is now (which if this has happened to you, you need to know that it's not ok for someone to force themselves on you – boyfriend or not.) When I went home, I was too ashamed and embarrassed to tell my family what had happened to me, and I didn't want to cause any kind of drama in reaction to what had happened. Despite what he had done, he was still my boyfriend, so I kept it a secret. This is where my first root of secret guilt formed.

A few weeks later, I began to feel sick, and discovered that I was pregnant. "Oh my God! What am I going to do?" was the first thing that came to mind. I was terrified to tell my mom who not only had already warned me about him but was also a ministry leader. I was afraid of what she would say. I was afraid of what my church family would say. When I think back on these days, I just remember being so scared.

I was scared of being judged, and I was scared of bringing embarrassment to my mom -- this powerful, faithful, and diligent woman of God who was a loving and selfless mother. I couldn't tell her that I was pregnant. I couldn't. It wasn't because I *couldn't* really tell her about my situation. But it was because I *believed* I couldn't, so I chose to keep it a secret. I'd even go so far as to say I was deceived into thinking that I couldn't tell her the truth. Now, I had a second root of secret guilt forming.

In the days that followed, I had no idea what I was going to do. I would cry night and day, and beat myself up asking the same question over and over "How did I allow this to happen to me?" Finally, the light bulb came on, and I knew what I had to do. There was one person that I hadn't told who really needed to know, so I took a deep breath, and picked up the phone to call the man responsible for the baby that was I carrying inside of me. I called my boyfriend.

Deep inside, I was thinking he would help make this right and then I could tell my family, but his response left me in total shock. "Oh no!" was his response. "You are not going to embarrass my dad and me! You cannot have this baby. You are going to have an abortion." He proceeded to tell me that he would take me to the doctor and pay for the procedure as if it was nothing to him. I was completely mortified, and I felt so lost and afraid. As I replayed his words in my head, I decided that he was right. This was the best thing to do. I hadn't thought about his dad, who was pretty prominent in the community, but I knew that I couldn't bear the embarrassment, or shame my mother or our church family, so when my boyfriend showed up to take me to the doctor, I got in the car, and went to the clinic. Without telling anyone where I was going, I followed through on having the abortion. Now, there was a third root of secret guilt formed, locked, and loaded.

Now, depending on what your beliefs are about women who have abortions, you could either say that what I just shared with you about my life is either not that big of a deal, or you could think I'm the worst person in the world for killing my baby. Either way, the purpose of this book is not to debate whether abortion is right or wrong, it's about the impact that holding secret guilt --- no matter what the source --- has on your life, and how hopefully you can avoid wasting valuable years of your life in bondage to it. Or if you're like me, and you're carrying a dark secret of your own, and a secret root of guilt has formed in your life as a result of something you did in the past, or something that happened to you, then you can learn how to come to terms with the past, and experience a liberating moment that births a season of complete peace --where the past no longer has a hold over you, and you can not only walk in freedom, but also become all that God has for you to be (and do) as you move forward with this next season of your life.

"Peace I leave with you, My peace I give to you; not as the world gives do I give to you. Let not your heart be troubled, neither let it be afraid."

John 14:27 NKJV

CHAPTER TWO

Unwanted House Guests

Little did I know that the medical procedure that I thought would fix my problem, and help me regain control of my life, would unleash so many other problems. When the guilt started (which was almost instantly), it was as if guilt was a person who knocked on the front door of my house, and when I opened it, he walked in, along with all of his friends – and their luggage—and decided they were moving in with me, without asking my permission. Guilt does this. It brings with it other emotions that you can't get rid of, as long as you allow it to stay. He brought with him anger, shame, depression, anxiety, and grief. They wreaked havoc on my emotions. Eventually, I started feeling disconnected from everyone and everything.

For a long time after it happened, I just cried day and night. I alternated between blaming myself and being angry at my ex, and I isolated myself from my family and friends. When they would ask "What's wrong?", I would pull myself together a bit and just play it off as if everything was ok, until I could get somewhere by myself. Then I would just cry, and ask myself, why did I kill my baby? In my mind, I could hear the devil's taunt, "murderer." The abortion was over, but all of the emotional pain that led up to the process (thinking it would fix the issue) remained, except now it was amplified. I had unwanted house guests living in my spirit, and I didn't know how to evict them. They were partiers, and they liked to be heard. Sometimes, they would go to sleep, but they were very light sleepers, and it didn't take much to wake them up.

As I reflect on that time of my life, I can honestly say I chose to have an abortion because I really thought it would solve my problems. I was so wrong. The problems increased. Every time I even heard the word "abortion", it would pierce my heart, and wake up Guilt, Shame, Fear, and Anger and they would start their party all over again. Every year, l would think about how old my baby would have been if it were alive. I wondered if it would've been a boy or a girl. And sometimes, when I went to church, I would hear a message on abortion. I hated those Sundays the most.

It wasn't often but when it happened – no matter how many years had passed since the incident – it would hurt so much inside. I'd feel as if my heart would explode. Oftentimes, I would make my way to the restroom until the sermon was over. I'd ease out my seat, and down the aisle, as smoothly as I could, hoping no one would notice me. This went on for years.

I wish I could tell you that time eventually healed my pain, and that it went away, but it didn't. It's what I wish I could tell the people who come to me for help dealing with some form of guilt. I wish I could hug them and say "It's ok. With time, it will heal." I wish I could say like the old saying "Time heals all wounds. "But it doesn't. Not the wounds of the spirit; not the wounds that guilt infllicts.

Ther are a few steps that you must take to find healing, and (Spoiler alert!) continuing to keep it a secret hoping that eventually the pain will subside and stop tormenting you -- is not one of the steps to finding healing. The pain may subside for a bit, but it's only sleeping. Eventually it will wake up and blindside you when you least expect it.

When something traumatic like what I experienced happens, you enter a denial stage at some point, or a numbing stage rather, where you just stop feeling anything at all for a while --- at least until something triggers the memories again, and all of the feelings awake, almost at the same time. My triggers were the word "abortion", passing the place where the abortion took place, driving near the place where the attack occurred, and having dreams about the baby that was aborted.

What are your triggers?

_____

_____

_____

CHAPTER THREE

Evicting Your Unwanted House Guests

I never understood why my journey to healing took so long. I think you'll agree with me that 31 years of holding onto what I considered to be a deep, dark secret is a very long time. Living with this ever-present feeling of guilt, and all of the baggage that came with it was stifling. I really don't know how I was living. I finally came to the point of realizing that healing is a process. When something like this happens in your life – that thing that was so bad that you just can't share it --- it's traumatic. To get past it, you have to remove the label of what you've given it --abortion, rape, abuse, molestation, incest, whatever your secret is -- and call it what it is, "trauma". Then you can begin to heal.

I asked a good friend of mine, La'Boris Cole, who's a counselor that's widely respected in her field to help us understand what trauma is and to share some insights with us. Here's what she shared:

"Trauma can be defined as one who's experiencing a life altering event that impacts someone physiologically and psychologically. Trauma does not discriminate. Trauma is not determined based on your race, your background, your belief, or even your profession. In life, you will experience some level, type, or extent of trauma. It is important to note that what you may experience or define as trauma may not be the same for another person.

To this end, trauma has a way of silencing your voice and/or displacing your emotions. To the person reading this, you deserve to use your voice despite what happened. You deserve to feel again. It is very appropriate to share your trauma with someone you trust, someone who has created a safe place to share your story, and someone who has proved that they can be trusted with your pain and discomfort. Remember, everyone does not deserve to walk on the journey to and through healing with you. There are a few angels on earth that were created to assist in providing a safe haven and strategies for you to walk through every traumatic event.

Don't be afraid to share your story to others. Share your story when you are ready. Share your story even if your voice shakes or trembles. Share your story with confidence. Share your story knowing that your story is giving someone strength and an extra push towards their destiny. You got this.

Dr. La'Boris Cole is a Licensed Professional Counselor in Dallas-Ft. Worth who specializes in addressing trauma. Visit www.LaBorisCole.com for more info.

Keep growing, glowing, evolving and do not forget to share your story! "

When you're dealing with secret guilt, there's a tendency to feel like you are the only person who's dealing with this, and that no one can help you. The truth is, you're not. For every bad thing that could have happened to you, or any bad thing you've done that's causing guilt, there are tens of thousands, if not hundreds of thousands of people – maybe even millions --- who've experienced it or done it, and there are counselors, the "heavenly angels on earth" that Dr. Cole referenced that can help with this.

There are also people who are anointed to pray with you, and help walk you through your healing. To receive healing, first you must acknowledge that something traumatic has happened and that you need God's help. You have to break the silence – not to a person first – but to God. You have to cry out to the Lord. This is where my healing began.

Growing up with a Christian foundation, my mother taught me the power of prayer at an early age but somehow, I seemed to have forgotten it while I was dealing with the reality of what had happened. I was caught in my feelings, and I wasn't talking to God during the times that I was busy reliving what had happened and blaming myself for what I'd done, all while battling guilt and shame. I was only focused on the pain. I was trying to live as best as I could --

putting on the best face possible for the world -- even though inside I was dying. Like a baby learning how to walk, I had to learn how to talk to God about my situation and what I was feeling. This played a big part in my healing.

I had to learn how to get into his presence. I would play worship songs, and I would share my real and very raw feelings. I'd be vulnerable and admit to him that what I was going through was hard and coming before him was hard. I'd ask for forgiveness for taking my baby's life, and for other things that happened. I began to read my Bible, and the scriptures would begin to minister to me. Scriptures like:

James 5:16:

"Confess your faults one to another and pray for one another that you may be healed"

Psalm 120:1

"In my distress, I cried unto the Lord."

Psalm 30:2:

"O Lord, my God, I cried unto thee and thou hast healed me."

My relationship began to grow with the Lord. Even though it was growing, I was not yet fully healed. I would still hurt from time-to-time about taking my baby's life. But now, I had more strength, and a place of solace and comfort. This gave me the power to start building up the strength to stare guilt in the face and begin the process of evicting my unwanted house guests.

CHAPTER FOUR

Staring Guilt in the Face

The guilt of an abortion (or whatever your issue may be) must be stared at and confronted. If you don't, you will not heal. It's not as easy as it sounds, but it can be done, and it must be done. There's no way around it, and with God's help you can do it. I'm reminded of some of the psalms that King David (who knew a thing or two about guilt and shame), prayed in Psalms 4:1 and 4:3:

1 Hear me when I call, O God of my righteousness: thou hast enlarged me when I was in distress; have mercy upon me, and hear my prayer...

3 But know that the LORD hath set apart him that is godly for himself: the LORD will hear when I call unto him

God will stand with you as you stare guilt in the face. I know firsthand the guilt and shame that's invading your life and the trauma that follows – maybe to the point of wanting to kill yourself (we'll talk about that later in this book). I know the anger and the struggle that you deal with in your mind as you're reminded of the bad choices you've made or the bad choices that someone else made that impacted your life. As a person who was date-raped as a young adult, I know what it's like to think someone is Prince Charming, and to later find out that he was the devil's son.

I know what it's like to be just starting out in the world thinking that you have it altogether, but inside there's a void, causing you to need validation from a man from where you didn't get it from your father, either because you didn't have one in your life, or perhaps you did, but he just wasn't there for you. Maybe he was too busy working to provide income for the family, or dealing with his own personal struggles like depression or alcoholism, and didn't know how to be a father to you, and as a result, you ended up being attracted to and trusting the wrong guy. Whatever the issue is, and whatever the reason you ended up in the situation that opened the door for guilt and shame to live in your house, nevertheless, it has happened, and you must be able to face it, stare at it, and admit, "yes, I did _____.

"If you're like me, and your secret guilt involves an abortion, you have to be able to say "yes, I murdered my baby." I know it sounds harsh, but it's only when you can say the truth about what happened, in the absolute harshest form, using the words that the enemy has been tormenting you with, and admit how hurt you are, how angry and painful this situation has been for you, and then give it to Christ, then and only then will the torment begin to break.

Believe me. It works. Stare it in the face, so that guilt can break off your life and it's required to take shame, anxiety, depression, anger and fear with it. If you don't, it will stay and continue to affect your life. Here's why:

The devil works in secrecy.

The Bible says he's the author of confusion/ chaos. Once you accept what happened, whether it's something that happened to you that was beyond your control, like a family member molesting you while you were growing up, or whether it was something you did, like have an abortion. It doesn't matter what the reason was, or how you came to the decision, what has happened has happened, and the choices have been made --- whether it was your decision or someone else's bad decision. Either way, the action has altered the path of your life, and allowed negative emotions to dictate your life, but you have control and can be set free.

Sometimes we get caught up in the details about the reason why we did something, and it keeps us from receiving closure and getting healed, and because we can't accept responsibility for what happened, it keeps us from getting free. Here's what I mean:

Let's say you became pregnant and started focusing on how the child was conceived. Maybe it was by force, so you make a decision that it's best to not have the baby. Or maybe it was a consensual act and the baby was conceived with someone who said he loved you. You thought you had something solid with him and a future together, but once he found out you were pregnant, he started distancing himself from you, and began acting differently toward you, so you decided to have an abortion because you couldn't raise a baby alone. Or maybe you conceived a child with a husband that you no longer wanted to be with or were unsure that the marriage would last. Maybe it was conceived with a man who you knew couldn't handle having to support one more mouth to feed, or you became pregnant when your kids were finally all in school, you were ready to get your life back, and having one more kid just would ruin everything, so you decided to have an abortion. At the time for each of these scenarios, your choice could've seemed like the right thing to do, so you took action – even if later you discovered it was a wrong choice.

Here's where the problem lies. We make the wrong choice, and we either can't accept it was wrong (because at the time it seemed really right), or we can't forgive ourselves for making the wrong decision. Either way, God wants to heal you, and he wants you to be whole. What's done is done. It's in the past, and you can't keep carrying the weight of the guilt. Jesus never intended for you to live that way.

Brothers and sisters, I do not consider myself yet to have taken hold of it. But one thing I do: Forgetting what is behind and straining toward what is ahead, 14 I press on toward the goal to win the prize for which God has called me heavenward in Christ Jesus.

Philippians 3:13-14 NIV

It's extremely important that you know as you try to escape your pain and those dark thoughts that only you and God know are there, that you have a God that wants and is waiting to rescue you from the level of guilt you feel. Christ came so that you can have life and have it more abundantly. He didn't come so that you can live in bondage to guilt and shame. It's time to get free.

The thief does not come except to steal, and to kill, and to destroy. I have come that they may have life, and that they may have it more abundantly.

John 10:10 NKJV

CHAPTER FIVE

Cutting the Umbilical Cord of Guilt

When a woman is pregnant, the umbilical cord feeds her baby. If you're a mother (or you've gone to High School or College where they talk about the human body), you know that whatever the mother eats, she feeds it to the baby through the umbilical cord. Well, guilt was my mother. It became like the person or the source that was feeding me, and what guilt feeds you is not good.

It's where all of the negative thoughts and the insecurities flow from. This is where shame, anger, and depression stem from. I'd even go so far as to say it's where overly passive behavior comes from (to the point where you become comfortable with verbal and physical abuse, stay in bad situations longer than you should, and are a magnet for negative situations). When guilt is your mother, it feeds you all kinds of unhealthy things, starting with the lie that:

- You'll never be forgiven

- You'll never be loved

- You're not good enough (low self-esteem)

And it also feeds you a very unhealthy dose of shame. But severing the umbilical cord of guilt is vital to your emotional, mental, and spiritual health. When you cut the umbilical cord, you are now separated from the lies and hurt that guilt has fed you, and you can live free.

Just like it's imperative for a doctor or mid-wife to cut the umbilical cord when a newborn baby enters the world so that it can live and grow, it's just as imperative for you to cut the cord of guilt and not allow it to remain. You may not be able to do it yourself, but God can. Allowing yourself to stay connected to the cord is like having a soul tie. Once you are connected to it, as long as you remain connected, it has a hold on you. It pulls on you and is able to control you. It also pulls you back into places you were once free from. This is why the cord of guilt has to be cut.

It will continue to produce negative things in your life, and all negative cords must be cut. Because whatever you are connected to controls you. Guilt desires to control your life fully. As long as you are connected to the cord of guilt, you are no longer in a place to discover who you are, because you have something else feeding you the false truth of who you are. By cutting the cord of guilt, you are now allowing God to become the person who feeds you. When God is your source, you begin to crave to drink and eat from his table --- from him, the life giver himself.

In Romans 8:37, he tells you that *"you're more than a conqueror."* In Psalm 37:25, he tells you, *"I never seen the righteous forsaken nor a seed begging bread"* In Psalm 17:8, he tells you that you're the apple of his eye and he hides you under the shadow of his wings.

Let God free you from everything negative that the cord of guilt has fed you. After you cut the cord, you will begin your healing process. It may not be easy at first, but as you give it to Christ, your fears, your thoughts of not ever being forgiven, or loved, or accepted, or good enough --- all of these negative emotions – must be given to him. He's waiting for you to release it to him. When you do, you'll be able to entertain healthy thoughts, which promote healthy emotions. Positive thought patterns can produce positive actions and put you on the road to a healthy recovery.

For Meditation:

He will never leave you nor forsake you. Do not be afraid.
Do not be discouraged.

Deut 31:8 NIV

CHAPTER SIX

Liberation Moment

A year and a half after that terrible incident, I met an awesome man who would soon become my husband (and still is today) in just six short months later. In love, and excited about the possibility of a great future with a great guy, I didn't want to think about my secret or the day that had plagued me every day of my life. I was growing in my relationship with the Lord, and getting stronger, and had finally found a sense of peace and happiness. I had pushed my secret as far back as I possibly could, trying not to remember that day, and I didn't want anything to ruin what I had with my soon-to-be husband.

I was growing stronger in the Lord, and with the distraction and excitement of true love for the first time, I felt better, but I wasn't healed yet. I wasn't healed enough to share with my fiancé the details of that day. I felt like it would ruin everything, and my worst fear would come true. He wouldn't accept me. I wouldn't be found good enough.

He would no longer love me, and I would feel the shame and anxiety that I had lived with every day, so I chose not to tell him. In my mind, not telling him seemed like the right thing to do, because it would only ruin the first good thing that had happened in my life in years. But, when truth was revealed, it turned out that not telling him was the same as deceiving him, which as you can probably imagine, didn't turn out well. It would've been better if I had told him upfront, and trusted God with the outcome.

Sometimes we take matters into our own hands to control the outcome, but the reality is the outcome belongs to God. In the Bible, when Mary was pregnant with Jesus, she was engaged to be married. It was not to her advantage (according to their customs) to have the child, or tell her fiancé that she was pregnant. But she told Joseph the truth. Even though it was a hard pill for Joseph to swallow, and he secretly thought about leaving her, God sent an angel to confirm that Mary was telling the truth, and that it was ok to move forward with his plans to marry her.

God still speaks today through angels and dreams, His word, and the Holy Spirit. If you're in a situation like I was, and you're struggling with whether you should tell your fiancé the truth, pray about it first and wait; then trust God with the timing and the outcome. If the one you're with is for you, he'll either accept you as you are, or if he's struggling with the truth, God will move on your behalf and it will work out. If he's not the one, he won't be able to accept it, and God won't move on your behalf, so that you can receive the right person who'll come along at the appointed time. It will hurt to lose the one that you're in love with, but in the end, it's only God's best for your life that you really want.

It was almost 20 years into our marriage when the truth came out about my secret. Even though I had a family, a husband and two beautiful children – both a son and a daughter that both turned out to be all I could ever want or dream of in a child -- I still hurt from taking my first baby's life. I often remembered that I would've had another child, an older one to my daughter and son. Very similar to how life was before I got married – when it was just me – I still couldn't share what I was going through or experiencing with anyone, especially now. My husband was a pastor, and I was the co-pastor.

Even though I was still dealing with my own secret guilt, God began to do something new in my life. I had developed this passion for women who were hurting. I would wake up in middle of the night crying and praying for young ladies. I'd be praying for women who were being abused, and those who had abortions –the same type of women that I now minister to through Brenda Barnes Ministries. Waking up in the middle of night praying over hurting women went on for so long, that it was becoming clear that God wanted me to help heal hurting women as my ministry.

My husband and I started pastoring a church called Victory Temple. On Sundays, we would open the altar for people to come and pray. Women of all ages would come to the altar, and as the Pastor's wife and co-pastor, I would put my arms around them, hear their stories and prayer requests, and I would weep with them. I could genuinely feel their pain. There were several who'd share with me that they'd just found out they were pregnant. Whenever those type of stories came to the altar, my love meter and passion would get ignited and go completely off the charts!

I'd encourage them to "have that baby and love that baby." I'd tell them it was going to be alright, but I couldn't find it in me to tell them that I had an abortion. After all, I was the Pastor's wife, and I didn't want to bring shame on my husband, just like I couldn't bring shame on my mom and our church family all those years ago. When I look back on all of this, I could also see another culprit at work in my life, pride. My heart would reach out for these young women, but I kept my secret intact. It wasn't until the day my daughter, Precious, came home and announced that she guessed she was a bad daughter because she was pregnant, that I had my liberation moment.

At first, my husband and I just stood there. Then I said, "Baby Girl, get your purse. Let's go to Wendy's," which was her favorite hamburger place. At a little table in Wendy's, I began to share my story and the experience that had haunted me for over 30 years, for the first time with anyone. As I shared the story of my pregnancy and the abortion, tears welled up in my daughter's eyes.

"Mom, you never told me," she said. "I know baby girl" was my reply.

I told her because I didn't want her to experience the guilt and shame that I carried for years. I didn't want her to endure the pain. That was the day that I was freed to expose the truth. It was the day that I was completely set free from the guilt of the past. As long as the secret is a secret, you're not free. It's not until you can share your story for the sake of saving someone else the hardship and suffering that you are truly free. I shared my story with my daughter but it was actually she who freed me by sharing she was pregnant. By her choosing to not keep it a secret and allowing me to share my story with her, without condemnation, but with showing compassion and accepting me as I was.

I shared with her because I saw that what happened in my life, could have happened in her life as well after she found out she was pregnant. It took courage for her to share the truth with me and her father that she was pregnant. It was the right thing to do. I know that it wasn't easy for her, knowing that her parents were pastors at the time, but I believe she stared the issue in the face, and she handled it. I didn't do that when I found out I was pregnant for the first time. And that's where Satan won in my life. On the other hand, my daughter accepted the truth; then announced it to us. In doing so, she was able to reveal her pregnancy and open up about it – ultimately freeing herself of the secret guilt that could have taken over her life.

This allowed her to establish a strong support team around her with her parents, her brother, and all of the other people who cared for and loved her without judgment. As a result, she produced something amazing in the earth --- a beautiful and talented little girl who lights up a room, and is blossoming into an incredible young lady. The world simply wouldn't be the same if she wasn't here.

With my daughter's secret now out in the open, the devil's army was disarmed, and my daughter was able to move forward with her life. He couldn't move into her house and taunt and humiliate her with guilt, like he did me. I wonder if I could have had the courage to do what she did when she became pregnant, if I could've walked in victory instead of defeat all of those years. On that day, in a little Wendy's restaurant in Dothan, Alabama, not only was my daughter set free to live her life, but her mom was set free to share the truth with my husband, my son, the church, and the women in my ministry. I had buried it for years until that moment, and now I was finally free! I was liberated to share with hundreds of women at women's conferences, and I got to see God at work. He had set me free, and now I get to be a part of the process of him setting others free. It's a very liberating moment when you get to help others get free from the very thing that plagued you for so long. It's worth the fight to get free.

I have no words for what it's like to uncover the guilt that I had dealt with so long. Prior to that moment, I knew that I had been forgiven of my sin because I had confessed it to God, and I had been drawing closer to him throughout the process. I was talking to God about the issue and handing him my pain, but I didn't share it with others. I never felt ready, or even able to share, until my daughter opened up to me.

In that moment, I immediately knew that I had to tell her. I felt as if the Lord was saying to me, "Now, share with her about your experience and let her know that she wasn't the only one who became pregnant. Tell her your story about how you became pregnant at 19, and was physically abused by someone and taken advantage of and everything that followed." After I shared that story with her, I also explained how for years I didn't want to think about what I had done, and couldn't even speak of it, but that day, in that moment, I stared guilt in the face and spoke about what had held me back for all those years. In that instance, God freed me – not just for me – but also for my daughter. In that moment, I was able to encourage her and give her life-giving instruction that I couldn't before.

I told her things like, "Hold your head up and forgive yourself after you ask God for forgiveness," and I reminded her of the truth of the situation, which was that she was about to have a beautiful baby boy or girl and give us a grandbaby, and that as her family, we were going to love her and the baby through this process, and that she was going to enjoy being a mom to her baby. She was able to walk away knowing that God and her family loved her greatly, and that she was going to make it through this.

This is what happens when you're able to stare guilt and anger in the face and overcome them. You become free to set others free. You can take the pain that you've gone through and your first-hand knowledge of what someone else who's going through whatever negatives you've gone through and get free (or even circumvent altogether) the havoc that guilt, shame, and anger will wreak on their lives so that they can live free. You then become free to encourage and guide and be that positive voice in someone else's life, that you didn't have in yours at the time secret guilt took root.

That's the reason we survive the bad choices that we make and the bad things that have happened, regardless of whether they were done by choice. It's not just because God is loving to some, and not to others, but because there is something for us to do after we survive the hard stuff. We are to go free our brothers and sisters, not to drown in secret guilt and have our voices silenced permanently. We are to free and empower those who have been in situations like the ones we found ourselves in.

On the day of the Last Supper as told in Luke 22, in verse 21, Jesus warns Simon Peter that Satan has asked to sift him like wheat, but he goes on to tell him that he (Jesus) has prayed for him that his faith will not fail, and that when he turns back, to go strengthen his brothers. Shortly thereafter, Jesus was betrayed and arrested, and Peter ended up disowning Jesus 3 different times, just as Jesus had told him that he would. Peter left and wept bitterly. He had to live with the guilt and shame of knowing that he had disowned the one who saved him, and the one he loved dearly, for the sake of his own safety. He had to live with the guilt of knowing that Jesus, who looked right at him when he denied him the third time, knew that he disowned him.

This did a number on Peter, and he had to deal with his battle of guilt and shame, until the time that Jesus healed him and restored him. At which time, he began focusing on strengthening the brethren, and became one of the greatest apostles. We're called to do the same. Satan may sift us like wheat as we live with the guilt of our choices or the choices of others, but we have a Savior on the throne who prays for us and is willing to restore us, but the restoration is not just for our comfort and freedom alone. It's also so that we can strengthen our sisters and brothers who have gone through what we've gone through.

Like Dr. La'Boris said, you have to share your story, even with trembling and shaking. Someone is waiting on you to get free so that they can receive their freedom. Take the next step to cut the umbilical cord and find freedom today.

Your Turn:

What is in your life that's staring you down; accusing you, reminding you, or lying to you? Whatever it is, stare it in the face, knowing God is with you, and tell it:

God has forgiven me of _____

- I'm free!

- I am loved by God.

- In the name of Jesus, you can no longer have control in my life. You can no longer win.

- In the name of Jesus, I bind the work of the accuser.

- In Christ Jesus, I am made new.

Therefore, if any man be in Christ, he is a new creature: old things are passed away; behold, all things are become new

For meditation:

Revelation 12:11:

And they overcame by the blood of the Lamb, by the word of their testimony.

Based on what you've gone through, and the secret guilt you hold, what type of people are waiting on you to get free, so that they can get free?

_____
_____
_____
_____
_____

What's stopping you from sharing your story?

_____
_____
_____
_____

Is there someone you know who is struggling with the same issue, who could benefit from what you went through?

_____

_____

_____

_____

_____

Take some time now to have a conversation with the Lord sharing your feelings about this and ask for your liberating moment.

_____

_____

_____

_____

_____

CHAPTER SEVEN

Grace or Opposition?

There are so many reasons why it can be hard to let go of secret guilt. Much of it has to do with our thoughts about people and how we think we'll be treated.

Sometimes, depending on what it is that we've done, revealing the truth could mean the permanent loss of something substantial like a position, our current source of income, a relationship with someone important to us like a mom or dad, a spouse, or a child. It may even be our freedom that will be at stake if the source of guilt is something illegal. It may mean public humiliation.

When we place a high value on people, reputation, or whatever it is that may be at stake, it's extremely difficult to allow ourselves to be vulnerable, and to let go of the very thing that's hurting us. When this is the case, you have to first take your fears and concerns to the Lord and wait for his timing. You should ask him to guide you on the when and what of how to get free, and who and when to share. Sometimes fears and concerns are valid. There may be negative reactions or some consequences to what you share. If things don't work out in your favor, you have to be prepared to accept them, knowing that the promise of Romans 8:28 *"in all things God works for the good of those who love him, who have been called according to his purpose"* is true for you.

It's important that you use wisdom when it comes to sharing and the timing. If a third party is needed as a mediator, or you need to seek the help of a qualified counselor to help you sort through this, then do what is necessary, but don't just go blindly sharing your secret to anyone.

When I first shared my secret with my husband, it was not as easily received as with my daughter. He felt betrayed and expressed that I had deceived him by not telling him prior to us getting married, and I withheld it for so many years after. It was a very difficult time in our marriage and took us a very long time to work through it. It wasn't a short process. It wasn't a painless process, and feelings were hurt on both sides in response to me taking the steps needed to get free, but we have gotten past it and he is one of my biggest supporters in writing this book to help others get free.

When it comes to living out what the Bible says

about confessing your sins one to another so that you may be healed, you have to know that confessing doesn't mean that everything will be perfect and everyone will celebrate with you, or that there won't be consequences for your actions, but when you can get to that place, it takes away the power of the devil and gives God something to work with.

If you're finding it difficult to let go of the guilt you're carrying where it's impossible to speak about it, there may also be another culprit at stake --- a silent culprit, pride. It's important that you and I understand the harm that pride can cause. It's also important to know what it looks like, and to spot it a mile away, so that we can cut it off. We must be able to identify pride and refuse to entertain it. We have all been guilty of entertaining it at some time or other.

It's sneaky. It can hide. It can disguise itself as logic or being smart, when it's actually a very dangerous thing that needs to be treated with the same seriousness as if pride was our opponent in a war. We have to declare war on it. If we don't, we'll fall into its trap. And when we fall into it, we walk on the path alone. In other words, Christ is not walking on the path with us. 1 Peter 5:5 says:

"God opposes the proud but gives grace to the humble."

Think about it for a second. He gives you grace if you're humble, but he opposes you if you're proud. Sometimes, it's very easy to be stubborn and stick with our feelings when we're proud, but you have to ask yourself the question I asked myself:

Which do you want from God....his opposition, or his grace?

If grace is what you want, it is vital that you lay aside pride so that God can work in our lives and we gain his grace and favor. Pride will have you constantly considering what others think about you. It continues to remind you of your flaws, when what we should be concerned with is what does God think about us. When I found out that I was pregnant, it was pride that wouldn't allow me to open up and share with the people that I loved.

When I had my abortion, it was pride that told me that no one could ever know. It reminded me that since I could never be forgiven of this sin, I'd better put a smile on my face to show that I was ok when I was dying on the inside. You'll know pride is there when you're more concerned with the fear of being judged than getting free of the pain. It causes you to walk in pretense. Maybe you know what I'm talking about?

Pride can make life very unpleasant. It is derived from fear of embarrassment or shame. For me, I'm reminded of how I chose to deal with pain alone to avoid others knowing what I had done. That may be you now --- walking in pride; holding that secret close to the chest, or so you think. That secret actually has you locked in the room with pride because you're concerned about how you will be viewed by others. You've made it about you, like I did. Pride will have you so consumed with yourself that it will completely engulf you and put you in bondage. Then it becomes all about your image. God wants to free you, darling. It has been a problem far too long.

When you recognize pride exists in your life, you have to kill it. If you truly want to kill it, ask God to do it within you, and He will. It's a humbling experience and may be painful to the ego and image, but God knows how to do it, and will. It's listed in the Bible as one of the things he detests, so he will help you get rid of it, if you really want it out of your life, and to please him. Avoid pride. Walk in God's grace, which is the favor of God. God will favor you and give you strength to get through any dark season in your life, but you must trust him. Let him free you through his love and his freedom.

"But he giveth more grace. Wherefore he saith, God resisteth the proud, but will give grace unto the humble."

James 4:6

CHAPTER EIGHT

An Inside Look at Guilt and Shame

Krista Smith

All have sinned and fallen short of the glory of God.

Romans 3:23

Everyone will experience guilt to some degree in their lifetime. None of us have really lived the full life we were designed to live, and we fall short of who we were created to be. According to Romans 3:23, *all have sinned and fall short of the glory of God.* It's clear. All people everywhere miss the mark.

Guilt can be thought of as both a state of being and a feeling. The Bible speaks of it as a state of being. When an offense is committed, we are in a state of guilt. Sometimes it may be unintentional, but we violate our own moral compasses as a result of living in a fallen world. When we are in a state of guilt, there is often an emotional response of self-reproach that is experienced. Guilt is now a feeling. When mistakes are made and the realization of guilt occurs, those feelings -- whether accurate or not -- can take over and convince us we are deserving of blame, bearing substantial responsibility for our own misconduct.

When a healthy sense of guilt is present, we benefit greatly. It tells us we have hurt ourselves or another. Healthy guilt is a reminder of our humanity and gives us the humility to admit our offenses and make amends. Healthy guilt acts as a reminder not to repeat the same action(s), to implement restraint and avoid pleasure-seeking behaviors. Paul talks about this as Godly grief in 2 Corinthians 7:8-11. Although his previous letter to the church at Corinth brought guilt, it was a guilt that led them to repentance; not the kind of guilt that was overbearing or identity-destroying.

Healthy feelings of guilt are needed to guide us in our relationships with God, ourselves, and others.

There are many benefits to be gained during this restoration and reconciliation process. Too often guilty feelings are not managed but pressed deep down. They begin to morph into secrets and false beliefs. The enemy's voice becomes louder as we neglect giving ourselves grace, mercy, and forgiveness. Our inmost being begins to erode as the feelings of guilt becomes toxic. Toxic guilt quickly becomes toxic shame. Guilt is about what I have done; shame is about who I am.

Knowing the grace and mercy that God freely offers us through Jesus that covers our sin, is a concept that seems impossible for many to grasp. Sometimes the idea that God forgives you is acceptable, but the ability to forgive yourself seems impossible. We are bound up by guilty feelings not allowing ourselves to be free of shame's damaging effects. The belief goes from, "I made a mistake!" to "I am a mistake!" "I did something bad!" transforms into "I am bad!"

In The *Gifts of Imperfection*, Brene Brown defines shame as "the intensely painful feeling or experience of believing that we are flawed and therefore unworthy of love and belonging." This will quickly become an identity the image bearer of God was never meant to believe, so we hide. We keep secrets. Unfortunately, this shame identity also presents itself when trauma or violence occurs. The victim has not done anything wrong and therefore is not guilty of wrongdoing.

The victim frequently takes on the shame of what has been done to him. Feelings of powerlessness and helplessness are often experienced. False guilt creeps in, and shame messages often emerge. The impact of the trauma perpetuates the shame-identity and vice versa. The tendency is to hide and keep secrets! When the shame identity emerges, the sense of self begins to spiral downward as each secret, distorted thought feeds another.

In *Letting Go of Shame*, Ronald Potter-Efron and Patricia Potter-Efron list the following examples:

- I am defective (damaged, broken, a mistake, flawed).

- I am dirty (soiled, ugly, unclean, impure, filthy, disgusting).

- I am incompetent (not good enough, inept, ineffectual useless).

- I am unwanted (unloved, unappreciated, uncherished).

- I am weak (small, impotent, puny, feeble).

- I am bad (awful, dreadful, evil, despicable).

- I am pitiful (contemptible, miserable, insignificant)

- I am nothing (worthless, invisible, unnoticed, empty).

Shame is one of the most powerful weapons Satan uses to destroy us from the inside out. Peter warns us that our *"adversary the devil prowls around like a roaring lion, seeking someone to devour."* (I Peter 5:8). He devours our very soul with the lies he whispers in our hearts and minds. Every word tears away truth and our true identity in Christ become less and less believable. These self-centered and self-absorbed lies lead to more and more hiding, more and more isolation, and more and more lies. The negative belief system becomes the driving force of our existence.

These shame scripts become automatic, and the cycle persists leaving a perception of hopelessness and self-doubt.

As that cycle spins, we manage our guilt and shame by developing a pseudo-sense of "self-protection." We hide our offenses from God, from others, and even from our own self. Carl Jung metaphorically describes shame as the "swampland of the soul." Toxic shame permeates every part of a person's being-physically, behaviorally, emotionally, relationally, and spiritually. Physically, shame operates below our logical, rational thinking. Initially, it triggers a noticeable biological response through the autonomic nervous system. Blushing occurs. There is a heaviness in the stomach. Respirations and heart-rate increase. This an inability to make eye contact. Shoulders may slump while the head is bowed. There is an intense amount of self-consciousness. Time seems to slow down. Thoughts and speech may be fragmented making it difficult to communicate. The fight, flight or freeze response can get activated. Fight response may come as anger, rage, defensiveness or arguing. Flight is the desire to disappear or an inability to respond.

Behaviorally, shame shows up in many ways. Addictions to illicit and prescriptions drugs, alcohol, pornography and sex, food, money, and power (to name a few) are problematic behaviors that have overly complex etiologies but are often fueled by shame. Anorexia and bulimia, perfectionism, anger and rage, defensiveness, and co-dependency are a few more of the many issues that are often rooted in shame-based identity. Shame also manifests itself in more socially acceptable forms like exercise, religious service, cleanliness, shopping, and working. These are healthy activities that can become unhealthy. It is important to examine the motive. If it is to prove value or worth, replace an unhealthy addiction, or become a way to assuage a perceived or real moral failure, it is possible shame is fueling behavior.

Emotionally, shame causes distress and undesirable feelings. Depression, anxiety, and low self-esteem are common issues. Shame-induced thinking could lead to feelings of anger at yourself or others, worry or fear, distrust, helplessness, unworthiness, embarrassment, inadequacy, worthlessness, and regret. To hide these feelings, some may portray themselves to be the opposite which is exhausting. Shame is also characterized by isolation, inferiority, and indifference. Many are inclined to suppress their feelings and emotions.

Relationally, shame is particularly disruptive. It seeks to hide and disengage. The natural consequences of hiding are isolation and disconnection. There is an unwillingness or inability to be vulnerable and authentic. At best, relationships are superficial. Walls are built where we are hidden behind anger, unforgiveness, passivity, fear, and self-loathing. Lastly, spiritually, shame is incredibly deceptive. Because of our inability to hide from our Father, false beliefs develop, severing us from the reality of a loving, gracious, merciful God. The lies of the enemy grasp the soul:

"The One who created me and knows me couldn't possibly love me!"

"I've gone too far, and His grace won't reach me."

"I cannot trust Him to love me just as I am."

"I'm defective, worthless, and unlovable-too broken, too disappointing and too despicable."

The oppressive thoughts steal our relationships, our joy, and our peace. David understood the oppressiveness and humiliation that unconfessed guilt and shame bring. Whether or not his affair with Bathsheba and the murder of Uriah were the source of Psalm 32:3-4, it is evident he knew the painfulness and isolation secret sin creates. He writes:

"For when I kept silent, my bones wasted away through my groaning all day long.

For day and night your hand was heavy upon me; my strength was dried up as by the heat of summer."

By becoming so focused on hiding mistakes and concealing shame-based beliefs, the true knowledge of our identity in Jesus slips away from our unconscious thoughts. As the days, weeks, months, and years pass, who Jesus says I am becomes more difficult to believe.

Denying, minimalizing, justifying, and rationalizing are all distorted thought patterns used to keep our shame pressed down and our secrets hidden. When the focus is on covering sin and shame, it becomes all-consuming leading to unrelenting weariness and exhaustion for the soul. The focus is on ourselves; we cannot see Jesus or others.

David went on to experience the consequences of his sin, but he tells how he overcame his downcast spirit in verse 5: *"I acknowledged my sin to you, and I did not cover my iniquity;*

I said, 'I will confess my transgressions to the LORD,' and you forgave the iniquity of my sin."

David confessed his secrets. He acknowledged to God the immorality he was hiding from himself and others and trying to hide from God. Toxic guilt and shame instruct us to hide, pretend, and lie, but the antidote is confession, authenticity, and truth. It is in this antidote that we find forgiveness, grace, mercy, and love from our God. David begins Psalm 32 describing how liberating and redemptive confession to God can be:

"Blessed is the one whose transgression is forgiven,

whose sin is covered.

Blessed is the man against whom the LORD counts no iniquity, and in whose spirit there is no deceit."

When there has been a struggle with guilt and shame, we tend to deceive ourselves about our own personal value and who we believe we really are. The concept of God also becomes distorted. It is common that shame-based thinking influences a belief that God is conditional, punishing, or distant. Challenging those beliefs about God's character, how He loves, and how He can be trusted is an important part of accepting our true identity in Christ. We are valuable, forgiven, and loved. *He is faithful to forgive transgressions and cleanse us from all unrighteousness* (1 John 1:9) just as he did for David. In Him, we find truth about who we are and who He is. There is great power in confessing to God. He already knows our transgressions and loves us still.

James 5:16 says, *"Therefore, confess your sins to one another and pray for one another, that you may be healed."* There is healing in telling your story to someone else. We confess to each other, and we pray for each other. There is healing in confessing and in listening. By participating in this process, we help each other grow. Shame will lie to you: "You're the only one! "You're the worst!" "No one will understand!" "If others know, they will detest me!" The only way to heal the lies that shame whispers is to tell the truth and expose the secrets.

When choosing that confidant, choose carefully. Look for someone who is spiritually minded, trustworthy, patient, humble, honest, and admits their own weaknesses. Safe people are people who are open to feedback and are growing in their own faith. Find that friend, a pastor, a minister, or a counselor. Consider support groups or small life groups that are safe places to discuss feelings and express needs. Find courage to disclose your secrets, all of them. When God's grace flows through others who can hear your story and meet you with love and grace, the lies you have been telling yourself are quickly discredited. Only then will shame begin to loosen its grip.

As you continue to deal with the aftermath of shame, it is important to recognize the negative thoughts that have become so automatic. Learning to identify how you are feeling and what thoughts are driving those feelings are key steps to overcoming this false identity. Explore those shame messages you hear and identify where they originated. Recognize who is telling you those messages now. Identify past and present events, behaviors, thoughts, and experiences that stir up those messages. Share what you discover with a safe friend. Untangling the lies and detecting painful patterns can sometimes be a very complicated process. Knowing why they are there and where they come from is a powerful weapon in moving forward. Seek help from a professional therapist when needed.

As you move forward with understanding, begin retraining your mind. Your identity is in God through Christ. Consider looking through His lens and lean on who He says you are. Search for what is true. Find the scriptures that work best for you. Write them down. Speak them out loud. Listen to God's voice. Become thankful! Focus on what He has done and what you have. Getting past the admission of guilt and shame is a difficult journey that calls for much perseverance, courage, and hard work. Seek Godly counsel and trust Him in the process. Give yourself time and grace and take care of yourself along the way.

When you can leave guilt and shame behind, there is so much joy in learning to love yourself. The amazing paradigm is that the inward focused thoughts and behaviors transform to an awareness of the brokenness and needs of others. By sharing and growing from our inward pain, we become outwardly focused and grow to be servants of God with pure hearts and genuine motives while understanding our own value and worth.

Krista Smith is a licensed counselor at a church in the Southeast. She works with individuals and couples in her community who are experiencing a wide range of mental health concerns, complexities, and emotional or relational turmoil. For more info, visit www.wcc.church/counseling or e-mail krista.smith.lpc@gmail.com

References:

Bradshaw, J. (2005). Healing the Shame That Binds You, Expanded and Updated.

Deerfield Beach: Health Communications.

Brown, B. p. (2010). The gifts of imperfection. Center City: Hazelden.

Caine, C. (2016). Unashamed; Drop the baggage, pick up your freedom, fulfill your destiny. Grand Rapids: Zondervan.

Cloud, H., & Townsend, J. (1995). 12 Christian Beliefs that can drive you crazy; relief from false assumptions. Grand Rapids: Zondervan.

Cloud, H., & Townsend, J. (1995). Safe people. Grand Rapids: Zondervan.

Gibbs, D. (2017). Becoming Resilient. Grand Rapids: Baker Publishing Company.

May, G. G. (2009). Addiction and Grace; Love and Spirituality in the Healing of Addictions. San Francisco: HarperOne.

Thompson, C. M. (2013). Th Soul of Shame. Downers Grove: Inter Varsity Press.

CHAPTER NINE

The Aftermath of Unforgiveness:

Unforgiveness is like Afterbirth. In case you're unfamiliar with what afterbirth is, let me explain. When a baby passes through a woman's womb, what happens next is called afterbirth. This is when the placenta and fetal membranes discharge from the mother's uterus. When this occurs, it's extremely important that the doctor or midwife remove all of the afterbirth from the mother's womb. If just a little is left, it's enough to cause an infection in the mother's body, which could lead to her death. Not that I'm trying to give you a medical lesson here, but this is what unforgiveness looks like when it sets in the heart. The heart becomes infected when you hold onto it, and it can lead to your death – emotionally, spiritually, mentally, and relationally --- even physically. It can affect your entire life.

I had to forgive the guy for what he did to me. When it came to him, I held onto unforgiveness for years. I didn't realize how the aftermath of what had happened to me, the afterbirth of unforgiveness were so similar. I didn't realize what a danger they were to the body and the heart. When it comes to unforgiveness, you must make a conscious decision to remove the unforgiveness in your life, just as intentionally and thoroughly as a doctor removes the afterbirth from a mother's womb. If you don't, it will kill you.

Unforgiveness creates a hardened heart. The infection of a hard heart is feelings of anger, resentment, bitterness, and hatred toward the offender, and somehow, it makes it easy for you not to forgive other people for lesser trespasses when they offend you. It creates buildup. If you're carrying unforgiveness in your heart like afterbirth, allow God to perform surgery on your heart and remove all of the hurts and pain that are the source of you holding on to unforgiveness so long. God is waiting for you to ask for his help and release it to him. I know this may not be an easy decision but it must be a conscious one. Unforgiveness brings harm to you; not the other person, so we must release all of it.

Like afterbirth, unforgiveness is poisonous. It's self-destructive and pollutes your spirit. According to *Unforgiveness and Your Health Counseling Directory*, diseases such as cancer are related to unforgiveness. 61% of cancer patients have forgiveness issues, suppressed anger and bitterness. Harboring bitterness in your heart brings consequences that affect you physically, mentally, emotionally, spiritually. Jesus speaks to us and tells us in his word to forgive

Unforgiveness Is Like Drinking Poison And Expecting Someone Else To Die From It".

Unknown

If you're struggling with unforgiveness, it's important to get free by taking this to the Lord. Here are some steps you can take starting today.

Step 1. Meditate on God's word daily (Mark: 11:25-26) *"If ye do not forgive, neither will your Father which is in heaven forgive your trespasses"* and Ephesians 4:32 *Be kind and compassionate to one another, forgiving each other, just as in Christ God forgave you. (NIV).*

Step 2. Put on some soft worship music and just allow it to minister to your spirit. You don't have to do anything. Just rest in him.

Step 3. Make sure that you release every situation and every person who has hurt you. This may not be easy and it may take you a long time before you can actually do it, but remember to ask God for his help. He hears you and he cares about you. He doesn't command us to do anything that he is not willing to help you carry out in your life.

"Give ear to my words, O Lord, consider my meditation. Hearken unto the voice of my cry, my King, and my God:

for unto thee will I pray. "My voice shalt thou hear in the morning, O Lord; in the morning will I direct my Prayer unto thee, and will look up. (Psalms 5: 1-3.)

Forgiveness maybe difficult for many of us, but I declare with God it is not impossible. Below you will find declarations for forgiveness to help you on your journey.

Declaration of Forgiveness:

Lord, I thank you and I declare that I will walk in forgiveness.

I declare that through you I am empowered to release all hurts, unforgiveness, pain, and anger.

Lord, I declare that in spite of how overwhelmed I become, you have yet forgiven me.

I declare your love is empowering me to forgive others.

I choose to release my hurts and the pains that have been done to me through others.

I declare and release all poison of resentment, unforgiveness, and anger from my life.

I declare and trust God to help free me!

I declare and choose to forgive myself through your eyes I declare I am loved. I am valued. I am forgiven.

I choose to put my past behind me, and I look

forward to the future you have in store for me.

I declare I am forgiven by you, and I am free! In Jesus' name, it is so! Amen.

CHAPTER TEN

Determining Freedom Over Your Life

If you're truly ready to get free, the first thing you have to understand is that freedom is a choice; you must fight for it. It doesn't come easy. I remember the struggle I had with waking up from day to day trying to drown the memory of killing my baby, while listening to the devil's replays reminding me constantly that I was a murderer. Living with the bondage of guilt and shame, I remember thinking I would never break free, but I did.

I had to make a conscious decision to find my freedom. I got tired of being held hostage by Satan. I could no longer allow myself to remain paralyzed in that dark place. I struggled in breaking free. I was constantly getting pulled back into that place of guilt and shame. You could say I was controlled by all of the guilt and anger I had about making such a bad choice and allowing myself to be pressured by this guy to follow through with it; all the while, thinking that I wouldn't be forgiven by God for taking my baby's life. That was a lot. I thought I'd never be happy or feel like myself again. I thought I'd never be free.

Your journey is different than mine, but just as it was for me, freedom is available for you as well when you come to the Lord with all of your hurt, all your feelings, and all of your fears, and choose to invite him into your situation and ask for healing and direction. When we stop being ashamed to tell our story or testimony for the sake of helping others, and embrace our healing, then freedom comes. But we must share it with people we can trust. Seek the Lord for wisdom and guidance to the right person and begin exploring your options.

Determine your freedom and fight for it. I had to stop entertaining guilt, and so do you. Freedom can be found. You must desire to be free. You must decide to walk away from your past hurts and the thoughts that seem to continually taunt you. It could be something you've been carrying since childhood. I want you to know that you can be set free.

Realizing the power of the freedom that you and I should walk in doesn't come easy, especially when you're dealing with guilt. Guilt must be dealt with. Stop ignoring it. Stand up against it. Conquer it. Stop denying it, for it is real.

Acknowledge where the bondage comes from and face it by declaring:

No more will I remain married to you. I divorce guilt, anger, depression, resentment, shame, (you name the emotion.) Tell it no more will I remain with you in secret. You are no longer welcome.

To find freedom I had to release it all, to rediscover who I was and what my purpose in God was. I wanted to know and embrace the plans that he had designed for my life.

For I know the plans I have for you, declares the lord. Plans to prosper you and not to harm you, plans to give you hope and a future.

Jeremiah 29:11

This is what God is offering you. It doesn't matter what you've done. He's waiting to free you of it all.

As far as the east is from the west, so far has he removed our transgressions from us.

Psalm 103:12

Are you ready to be free? Stop allowing guilt to hold you captive because of fear. It must be arrested. Fear has a way of talking you out of your freedom and blessings.

We start believing the negative report and negative emotions instead of believing God's truth. God wants us to experience his freedom.

I'm reminded of the story of the twelve spies sent to Canaan found in the book of Numbers. The men replied, "Those people are much too strong for us." They started spreading rumors and saying, we won't be able to possess the land, for the people are like giants. Both Caleb and Joshua stood against the opinion of the spies. (Numbers 13:25-32). Basing their report on a firm commitment to God and full confidence in his promises to Israel, they refused to accept the overwhelming decisions of God's people even at the risk of their own lives. As a result, Caleb and Joshua possessed their freedom.

The people who listened to both the spies report, and Joshua and Caleb's thoughts on the matter had a choice to make as well. They could have given in to fear and missed out on their blessing, all the beauty and freedom of the land God had promised, or they could choose to overcome the fear of their giants and walk in freedom also. Fortunately, they realized later that they needed to overcome their fear and unbelief.

What giants do you need to overcome to walk in your freedom? Whatever it is that appears to be the giant in your life that's stopping you from your freedom, you can defeat it, for as Joyce Meyer says, the battleground is in the mind. Dismiss the fears, shame, guilt, disappointments, and whatever it might be and claim your freedom. Freedom is always connected to truth. Be truthful to yourself and choose freedom. Choose to see freedom instead of your giants. God said he wants you free. Obey his word. Truth is found only in his word. Trusting God is the antidote to fear, guilt and unbelief.

You will know the truth, and the truth will make you free.

John- 8:31-32

Your Turn:

Write 3 things in your life that appear as giants stopping your freedom:

1.

2.

3.

Repeat these declarations over your life daily:

• I declare that I'm made whole. I'm no longer tied to my past hurts. "My faith hath made me whole." Matthew 9: 20-22

• I declare I will overcome every obstacle, outlast every challenge, and come out of every dark place that has held me in bondage. I declare freedom has come. In Jesus' name.

• I declare Ephesians 3:20 over my life. God will do exceedingly and abundantly above all that I could ask or think. I have found healing for every wounded place. I no longer dwell in my place of pain because Christ is my healer.

- I declare I am not just a survivor. I am a thriver. I will bounce back from every trial. God's favor is on my life.

- I declare I am more than a conquer, and that all things are working for my good.

The following are some declarations to help you walk in freedom. Speak these over your life every morning or night. These are great for sharing with your family as well.

Prayer Of Declaration

Lord, Jesus:

I declare that I am free of any secret guilt and shame.

I declare that my heart and mind are healed of all past hurts.

I declare that I increase in your love and peace. I declare I am forgiven and that I forgive.

I declare that I have a new beginning in Christ Jesus.

I declare that I will use my pain for purpose to help others who are experiencing similar hurts.

I declare that all attachments of guilt and shame are broken off my life.

I declare that I am who God says that I am.

I declare that I am fearfully and wonderfully made.

I declare that I have the ability to forgive myself.

I declare that I don't drown in my pain.

I declare that Jesus promises to never leave me, nor forsake me.

I declare that whom the son sets free is free indeed. In Jesus' name I pray, Amen!

CHAPTER ELEVEN

But You Don't Know What I've Done

Depending on what has happened in your life, you may be thinking, "Brenda, this whole idea about finding freedom from guilt and making your declarations is nice, but it's not going to happen for me. You don't know my story."

If I were there with you, I'd admit you're right. I don't know your story, but I do know that there's nothing you could've done, no matter how vile, that God can't forgive or heal. From ministering to so many people over the years, I've learned that when a person says, "but you don't know my story," what they are really saying is "What I did (or what happened to me) was so bad that I'll never get over it and I just can't let it go." What happens when you take this position is you're putting yourself above God, and you're holding on to something that has the power to destroy you. Instead of confronting the issues and fighting for closure so that you can file this away in your past, you've now given guilt, shame, and unforgiveness license to wreak havoc in your emotions. You've made yourself a judge and decided that what Christ is willing to forgive you of, you don't deserve it, and therefore, won't forgive yourself. It can evolve to the point where you unconsciously choose to keep reliving the pain, over and over again – whenever it chooses to strike -- and you live this dysfunctional life, never allowing yourself to fully mature to a place of personal growth and complete freedom. You either do that or you let it torment you to the point where you find yourself entertaining the thought of taking your life as a solution for ending the pain.

Neither produces good fruit in your life. Both rob you of your future. They rob you of the chance to evolve into this amazing future version of yourself who's buried underneath the layers of pain and accusation, just waiting to emerge. It's the version of yourself that is healed and set free to discover her full potential, in spite of her past, in spite of her mistakes to become all that God created her to be and do.

So, what if the act that occurred in your life is so bad you feel as if you'll never be truly free of both the shame you've been secretly dealing with, and the shame you believe is sure to come once the world knows what happened? What if what happened is so terrible, or so life altering that you just don't see how there's any way out, except to end it all and commit suicide? What do you then? Should you do it?

Like a whisper, I'm sure the thought comes around

every once in a while (and some days more than others) that if you take your life, it will solve everything, and the people around you would be better off. Or maybe it's presented in a thought that no one cares, and you have no one anyway, so go ahead and end your life. Sometimes that thought is just a fleeting thought, and sometimes it comes in waves --- to the point where you're certain that it's the right thing for you to do.

You've tried drinking your way through it or getting high to drown out the thoughts. You've tried sleeping your way through it or doing the exact opposite and stay busy every waking second of the day so that you don't have time to think about what has happened (and when you stop the thoughts sometimes blindside you) or you're like many people I know and depression is your constant state.

During these times, you feel absolutely hopeless, and ending it all (in some way) is both a torment and a comforting thought all at the same time. Maybe this is something you've been entertaining for years. Maybe it's something that you've just started thinking. Regardless of what coping mechanisms you use to deal with guilt, and what actions you're taking when the thoughts come around, the thought is there nevertheless, and it's there more than you'd like it to be.

I don't know your story. I don't know what you're dealing with or what your world will look like if your secret gets out, but there are a few things I do know. If you give me a few minutes, I'll share them with you.

1. Suicide is a permanent solution to a temporary problem.

When you decide to end your life, it's permanently over, and at first, this may sound great. But if you really think about it, it's not your life that you want to end. It's the pain and despair, the hopelessness and feelings of worthlessness, the shame, humiliation, the fear – and whatever else you may want to end. I can tell you from experience. No matter how long you've been dealing with those feelings, they will not last forever, if you determine in your heart to confront the issues and take the steps to make it happen. I'm reminded of Romans 8:37:

> *Yet in all these things we are more than conquerors through Him who loved us. ...*

2. There are other ways to make those feelings go away permanently, besides taking your life. It's not your only option.

There are ways to make the feelings stop, without cutting off all the great things that are on the other side of this huge boulder or wrecking ball, rather, that has come through your life. You may not feel like this today, but you have a lot to offer the world. You're unique in ways that the world needs, and you were made for a purpose (not just so you can suffer and die, but to overcome and live, and leave your mark on this world. Depending on what type of life you've lived and what choices you've made, your mark may not be known as a good thing at this stage of your life, but with Christ's help, you can turn it around. He has been helping people in bad situations get a fresh start for centuries. You're no exception. He knows how to help you navigate. There's joy and peace on the road ahead, but first you've got to deal with the issue that's causing the pain and the suicidal thoughts. Suicide is never the solution. It's truly a permanent solution to a temporary problem.

Do you remember the umbilical cord we discussed earlier? One of the things that guilt feeds you – in addition to an unhealthy dose of shame – is a steady diet of suicidal thoughts. It gives birth to it, and they flow all around you, until you can't help but to think it's the way to go. If you entertain the thought long enough, you'll eventually begin to think it's true.

It's like watching one of those bad infomercials that come on late at night, trying to sell you something you don't really need. You know the ones. They play for a really long time.

During these shows, there's a story that's being set up. There's a storyline being fed. Someone is setting you up for what they want you to believe, and an action that they want you to take at the end – regardless of whether it's in your best interest or not.

Unhealthy guilt is like that. It's a tool the enemy uses to cut off your entire future and rob of you of your best self. Who you are today is not who you will be in the future. The way things are today is not how they will be in the future, and the pain you feel today, will not be with you in the future, if you take the right steps and make a commitment to getting free through the power of Christ and those who have been trained or equipped to help with what you're going through.

You can do this by:

• Admitting to both yourself and God that you need help, and you can't do this on your own.

• Asking Christ for assistance, healing, wisdom, clarity, and strength to get past this season of your life, and to give you a fresh start (and we'll talk about what that might look like in a few minutes.)

• Submitting your fears and thoughts to the Lord about the issues that you perceive are the realities of your situation. (In other words, whatever the issues are surrounding your situation that make death a more attractive option than living, these are the issues to submit to Christ.)

• Praying for the right people to help with what you're struggling with.

• Begin interviewing (or getting to know) people to determine if they're qualified to help with what you're trying to kill in your life once and for all, without taking your life. This may be someone who's a medical professional. It may be a pastor or person in ministry who has firsthand experience and revelation about what you're going through (even if they haven't shared it publicly), or it could be a good friend, or someone like myself who was given the gift of prayer to help clear the way for others.

3. There is healing available through Christ.

Sometimes it comes supernaturally, with just you and him. Sometimes he uses people who are skilled in counseling, therapy, or people that have been given the spiritual gifts of encouragement, teaching, and intercession (prayer) who come across your path with a message that speaks right to you, or a friend to come alongside you and speak just the right word to your situation at the right time, or pray on your behalf when you don't have the strength or the words to pray on your own.

Even if you don't see it today, even if you don't believe it today, the world needs the healed and free version of you. They're waiting on you to get healed and for the real you, the best you, the version of you who has fought her demons and won, off-loaded their baggage and is ready to make her mark on the world to come forth. Regardless of what has happened, there is always hope. There is healing available to you.

For I know the plans I have for you," declares the LORD, "plans to prosper you and not to harm you, plans to give you hope and a future. Then you will call on me and come and pray to me, and I will listen to you. You will seek me and find me when you seek me with all your heart.

Jeremiah 29:11 -13

The thief comes only in order to steal, kill and destroy; I have come so that they may have life, life in its fullest measure.

John 10:10

In the news over the past couple of years, I've noticed an increase in younger people in their 20's and 30's committing suicide. What made me pay attention is that many of them were seemingly successful and seemed to have a lot going for them. I remember hearing a story of this young lady who reached the peak of her career.

She held the highest position in the corporation. She was beautiful, smart, and ambitious and was without a doubt, by all standards, what we would call very successful. She had everything going for herself. But later we learned that this beautiful, successful young lady committed suicide. As hard as it was for us to believe, she took her own life, leaving us wondering -- after all these accomplishments -- what could have driven this beautiful lady to suicide, or any of these other people that we hear about? I wonder if guilt or shame could have dealt any of them an unfair hand and played a role in them taking their own life?

We'll never know the answer, but what I do know is there is nothing so bad you can do that justifies you taking the precious life God gave you. You may have mismanaged your life. You may have taken a wrong step, done something vile, or been dealt something unfair that was beyond your control. You may not be able to undo what was done, but I can assure you, your life is worth fighting for. Jesus thought so. He proved it when he decided to go on the Cross to die for both you and I, and chose to forgive us of our sins, so that we could have life and have it more abundantly. If he thought it a worthy enough cause to give up his life for you, then your life belongs to him. He purchased it, and it's not yours to take.

If you're contemplating taking your life, whatever life you chose to live, no matter the mistakes, no matter the addictions, no matter the habits that you have, no matter the injustice, no matter what was done, Jesus is willing to heal, and he knows how to help you navigate what seems like an absolutely impossible situation to recover from to help you get a fresh start, free of guilt and shame.

Your fresh start may mean you have to confess something that you don't want to share. It may mean you have to move. It may mean that you're going to lose some people and things that matter to you. Or maybe you have already. You may have lost all of your friends. You may have lost this and lost that, but Jesus can be the answer for you right where you are at this present time. He can restore back to you. He can show you his purpose for your life, and things that you never dreamed of. But when you turn to him, he can take you by your hand and take you farther than where you are now to a new season, new people, new opportunities. He's not in the business of leaving his children stuck.

Your fresh start may mean you have to start over in a new career or a new town and with new people. It may mean you're going to be uncomfortable. You may have some hard times ahead, but God knows how to help you rebuild a great life and bring the right people into your life. It hurts when you can't depend on the people you used to turn to, or you're excluded from things that used to matter to you. In Psalm 68:6, it says, *"God sets the solitary in families"*, so if that's what's missing in your life, he can provide even that. Your fresh start may mean that first you have to face some consequences that you'd rather not endure, but if you ask, God will be with you. He will give you the strength and the courage you need to face it, and he'll walk with you through the fire and to the other side, if you ask.

Your only job is to forgive (whether that's yourself or the offender) and to trust Christ to do what he does, which is help you navigate this season of your life and to help you rebuild your life for his glory. He specializes in giving beauty for ashes. He has been doing it for generations. You're not the first person's life he has had to restore. I'm living proof. There is hope at the end of the tunnel. Jesus is that hope. Give him that hurt, that problem, that disappointment, that fear, the addiction, the distrust, whatever it is. Give it to him and watch him turn it around.

He cares for you. He cares about you, and he wants you to know he loves you beyond what you've done or what has happened to you. He wants you to give him all the guilt, the shame, the hurt, the pain and the disappointment that flares up at times to cause you to even think about taking your life. Suicide is not the answer. When you're going through something alone, it's hard to imagine that you are not the only one who has done what you've done, or experienced what you have gone through, but truth is, there is always someone who has done worse than what you've done, and experienced worse than what you've experienced.

I know life can be unbearable sometimes, but when you understand that there is nothing so bad that you could do to take your life, and that there is nothing that Christ can't forgive you of.....and when you realize that Christ is for you, and not against you, then you can find the strength to approach him in humility and ask for his help and healing for this thing that seems bigger than you, and watch him wipe out the thing that tears at you and makes you feel worthless. Meanwhile, if you need someone to talk with by phone or chat about how you're feeling, contact our friends at the:

National Suicide Prevention Hotline at 1-800-273-8255.

I may not know your story, but I do know that healing and forgiveness is available to you, and nothing is too hard for Christ. No matter what you've done, or what has happened, our God is a Redeemer and the God of fresh starts. You have more to live for. Let him show you your value and your purpose.

Therefore, if anyone is in Christ, he is a new creation. The old has passed away; behold, the new has come.

2 Cor 5:17

Commit your way to the LORD; trust in Him, and He will act...

Psalm 37:5

If any of you lacks wisdom, let him ask God, who gives generously to all without finding fault, and it will be given to you.

James 1:5

CHAPTER TWELVE

Finding Forgiveness in the Courtroom

While I was working on the manuscript for Secret Guilt, I found myself sitting face-to-face in a courtroom with a man who had been accused of sexual assault to a minor. I had been drafted for Jury Duty. I was praying that they wouldn't select me, because I knew it was going to be difficult for me to be objective in this case. Meanwhile, I was sitting right across from the accused. Right on the second row. Right in front of him. I was also sitting right across from the plaintiff, the young lady who accused him of the act.

They were both younger at the time of the alleged crime, but for some reason the case was just coming to trial, some years later. As the lawyer began to share the details of the case, it was pretty simple. The guy was being accused of assaulting the young lady when she was a child. Not that it mattered, but the defendant was also much younger when it happened as well.

As I listened to the lawyer, I immediately came to a conclusion about him in my mind. "Yes, he did it," I said to myself. The more I looked at him, "Yes, he's guilty!" Mind you now, I had not heard all of the facts or even seen any of the evidence. This was just the beginning stage where they were briefing us on what the case was about before they began their juror selection. My heart went out for this young lady, and I began to pray for her within my spirit, and I felt her pain. She had already gotten my vote because I had a flashback of what happened to me when I was 19. The details of the case were somewhat similar to my past experience, and I found myself being reminded of all the feelings I had. I became overwhelmed with emotions as a result of all this.

I heard the full details of the case. Then the lawyer began to ask us if we could be fair in this case after hearing all of the evidence. He reminded us that the person is innocent until proven guilty, even though in my mind, I had secretly already convicted the man. The lawyer continued to proceed. He wanted us to let him know if we would be biased in any kind of way. If so, they needed to know. We were asked to line up and go to the back of the room to share with the judge our concerns, while the attorneys listened. The whole time I'm in line, I'm still thinking about the young lady and what she might have experienced. This only continued to stir up my emotions and bring up memories of my past.

It was now my turn to share with the judge my feelings about the situation. I immediately began to tell him that I didn't think I could serve as a juror and not be biased because I lived through something very similar to this case. I also shared that I have a Women's Ministry for hurting women that are in this same type of situation, and that I was very passionate about this type of thing.

To make sure there was no confusion about my inability to fairly judge this case, I went on to tell him how I believed God called me to bring healing to women who were wounded from being taken advantage of and were dealing with the aftermath of physical abuse and sexual assault, including the guilt and shame that comes from it, and I shared with the judge that the defendant was already guilty in my eyes.

The judge and attorneys thanked me for my honesty. The judge sent me back into the courtroom until he finished listening to the other jurors. "Done! I'm home free. Nothing left for me to do here, but wait to go home," I thought. Well, at least I thought there was nothing more for me to do.

Stepping back into the courtroom, I returned to the same seat where I was sitting earlier. Right in front of me was the defendant. He was sitting at the table alone facing us. The attorneys and the young lady had all left the room. He was just sitting there looking around.

Before, I had left the room to talk with the judge, I had no love in my heart for this guy. All I could see was my attacker and he represented him, and every guy who had hurt the women I minister to. The only person's pain or heart, rather, that I could feel was the alleged victim, and my own. Now, as I'm waiting for them to tell me I can go, I began to feel something tugging at my heart as I looked at this man. I was staring at him. Then I began to think about how he must feel sitting there knowing that he was being judged before his case was even pleaded, and we had never even heard his side of the story. Then I heard the Lord say, "That used to be you."

You would think he was referring to me as being the young lady, right? But he wasn't. She had left the room. He went on to say, "At one time you were afraid to share what happened because you felt so much guilt and shame of being judged by others, and what they would say or do if you opened up and told them what happened to you, the assault, becoming pregnant, and then pressured into having an abortion. That was you at one time. It took you almost 30 years to share your story."

He reminded me that he came to my rescue and took the guilt away from me and how he freed me of all the heaviness I carried from the guilt of my choices. Then something unexpected occurred. My heart was now broken for this man sitting before me now. Not to say that he didn't commit the crime, or to take away from what he did, but this man needed to at least have the opportunity for his case to be heard. I could literally feel this man's pain, knowing that he felt alone and judged. God said to me this was all of us at one time in our life. We were guilty of judgment, so he sent his son to die for us, to free us of all guilt and shame.

I'm not saying that this man was innocent, and that he didn't deserve punishment, but even if he was guilty, he still needed to be shown some kind of mercy. He needed to know that God still loves him, and is there for him, in spite of the situation he has found himself in --- whether he was there because of his own wrong choices, or whether it was because he was being falsely accused. Either way, he needed someone praying for him. So, by now I'm trying to hold my crying in, so as not to create attention to myself, and I started truly praying for this guy. It was at this point that I was reminded, isn't this what your book is about, getting free from guilt and shame and not drowning in your shame? This was no doubt his secret guilt; her secret guilt as well.

I had the heart for the young lady. I wanted to help heal her. I wanted to hug her before listening to the conclusion of the case. I had already pronounced him guilty, but God reminded me of my assignment of writing this book and using this as a tool to bring freedom to all, no matter female or male, black or white, Hispanic, Asian, no matter your ethnicity and no matter what the source of guilt was. God is no respecter of persons. He doesn't assign values or levels to the sins we commit, or the hurtful things that happen to us. He's not like us, where we decide one thing is worse than the other. He wants us all free from the effects of guilt and shame. It was never our lot to have in life, but a result of us living in a fallen world, and thus the need for a Savior.

I'm now looking at the guy with tears in my eyes. I pulled out this large piece of paper and begin to write in big letters, "Jesus loves you". I still can't believe I did that. I held up the paper in front of me, where he could see it – trying not to draw attention. He read it. Then his eyes begin to tear up. He halfway smiled, closed his eyes, and nodded his head as if he was saying, "Thank you." I quickly folded up the piece of paper and put it back in my purse just in case someone stopped and asked me about it. That day I learned an important lesson. Show love and mercy and allow God to show love to people through you, no matter what a person has done.

If you find that you can't forgive or show love to a certain type person, here are some steps you can take:

1. Ask God to help you see this individual or type of individual through God's eyes.

2. Admit that you're having a hard time forgiving and ask him to help you to forgive. Pray on a regular basis about this until you feel your heart soften towards them, remembering Matthew 6:15 that if you do not forgive others their sins, your Father will not forgive your sins, and also remembering that we once too, were guilty of judgement before Christ rescued us.

I felt the man in the courtroom needed to be free of the guilt he was carrying regardless of the outcome of his case. We need to remind people of who God is, and what his thoughts are toward them. We need to forgive and remind them that God still forgives and heals. It's not our place to judge their sin. It is our place to redirect them or connect them to Christ, and it's our job to forgive. The outcome is up to God. This is what freedom looks like.

CHAPTER THIRTEEN

Parenting and the Guilt We Dish

During my liberating moment with my daughter, it was a great moment in our relationship. I was able to say the words she needed to hear to feel strengthened and supported, and to be encouraged to not only have her baby, but also know that there was hope on the other side of what could easily be seen as a terrifying and life-altering situation for a young woman who was popular with dreams, ambitions, and a bright future ahead of her. As a result of being able to be there for, to speak life over her, and be the mom she needed me to be, she was able to plan and move forward with her life without having to experience the bondage that millions of young women in her same situation face when they have to navigate something of this proportion alone.

I was able to give to my daughter what she needed as her mother because God helped me find the courage to finally open up about my experience and share what needed to be said in that moment so that she could live free. I wish I could say that I've always handled situations that well with my children, but I haven't. And over the years, ministering to hundreds of young women who've found themselves in all types of bad situations, I've heard horror stories of how parents have failed their kids. They've single- handedly given guilt the keys to move into their children's lives because of their own expectations, fears, or pride; not really giving any thought to the child and what they may be feeling. In other words, it's about them (the parent), not the child. I can remember two such occasions where I was guilty of this. I was the main culprit dishing out the guilt, and I remember the effect it had on our children. One involved Precious.

When Precious was growing up, I was a Stay-at- Home mom. In fact, I had always been a Stay-at-Home mom. My husband, Napolian, who is an awesome provider, made that possible from the time we had our first child. As young parents, we wanted to do everything right, beginning with their foundation. Our goal was for me to stay home to make sure our children were loved, properly taken care of, and that we instilled a strong Christian foundation in them. He and I raised – a son (Napolian, Jr.) and a daughter (Precious) who were born 5 years apart. As perfect as all of this sounds, don't get me wrong. I'm not saying that it was easy all of the time. I'm not even saying that we were perfect parents, because the truth is half the time, we were trying to figure out how to parent our children, and a lot of times we got it wrong. I told you about the time that I did it right with Precious, so it's time I tell you about the time I got it wrong.

As a parent, I had very strict rules for our children. I grew up in a strict home. My mother was my role model. She was loving. She was so loveable. I remember all the kisses and hugs she'd give, and how she kept us on our knees praying. Even though it got on my nerves, and I didn't appreciate all that praying that much as I was growing up, she was still such a Godly role model. She was also strict. You could describe her as being one who "didn't play" when it came to us girls and foolishness. She and our dad had divorced early, so without him being in the home, she made sure we understood that she was the one in charge. At the end of the day, my mom was amazing. I didn't feel that way growing up, but as I got older, I realized just how amazing she was, and what a blessing it was to be with her. So, when it was my turn to raise kids, I decided that I would try emulating Mom, because after all, she was the best role model I could have.

She showed us and the rest of her family so much love. She was a prayer warrior, and a selfless person, so I didn't have a problem learning those things as a parent. But what I didn't learn from her, or know how to do, was how to listen to our children or understand how important it was for them to be heard and be able to express themselves, correctly, without being punished for it. Growing up, my siblings and I were not given an opportunity to express ourselves. Well, I expressed myself, of course, as I mentioned in a previous chapter. I had to pay a price when I did. Speaking about how you felt about something as a child or teenager was considered as "sassing your parents" so I had nothing in me that said I should be listening to or letting our kids express themselves beyond what I was personally comfortable with accepting.

So here I am, a mom to this beautiful teenager, who was not just my daughter, but a very sweet and smart young lady. She was an Honor student, and very likeable. She was so likeable she was voted Miss Homecoming Queen. Now she was in RN school at the top of her class. As a Preacher's Kid (PK), she was also very faithful to the work of ministry, and she loved the Lord. She was a really great kid, so what more could I ask for, right?

Well, as a Born-again Believer I held beliefs that we couldn't watch certain things or play certain games. One particular day, Precious was in her room enjoying some down time and playing a game on her computer. I can't remember the name of it, but the game had this weird face on it, which I found unsettling. I didn't trust what was behind this game, and I didn't like it, so I barged into the room and snatched it.

She started trying to explain the game to me. But listening to what my kids had to say after I made a decision was not my strong suit. As a result, things blew up and words were exchanged. That situation didn't have to escalate like this, but me being the way that I was when it came to parenting, I only thought of myself and my feelings. I gave no thought to how she was feeling.

This situation and how I handled it, scarred my daughter for years, but God dealt with me on the issue and showed me years later that I needed to let go of my pride and fix this with my baby girl. I had to apologize to her and admit that I was wrong, and actually hear her out. This was very vital to restoring our relationship. As she began to share and open up to me, expressing her hurts, tears began to run down her face. I remember embracing her tightly and sharing how sorry I was, and the hurt I felt as listened to the pain that I caused her. I had to heal my baby girl.

It was through humbling myself and admitting I was wrong that our relationship began to get stronger. I realized that as an Evangelist and Co-Pastor, I couldn't heal the world and let my child bleed out. No! It was imperative I healed that wound with my love. It's love that heals a wounded place. As parents, our responsibility to our children is to love, teach them the word of God, correct in love when needed, give them to God and be patient with them. And if we are the ones who cause them pain, to humble ourselves and fix it. Unfortunately, I had to learn the hard way that as parents we have to be willing to admit when we don't know a certain thing, and when we're wrong. If we want a good relationship with them, we must learn how to listen and treat them as individuals, a person with feelings. I had to learn this early on with my son as well.

If you know anything about PKs (Preachers' Kids), you know that they are the most pressured kids around because they are held to such a higher standard. They are constantly under a microscope, whether they're at church, at school, the grocery store, the movies, it doesn't matter. They're human just like any other child, but they are constantly judged (and often misjudged) by many. Unfortunately, they're also targeted the most by the enemy, and are often robbed of their God-given identities and purposes because of parents in ministry who want them to be who we think they should be.

If you've never been a PK or been besties with a PK, you may think the challenges of being a PK are overstated, but I can assure you, there's always something expected of them, and I've seen many pastors overlook the fact that PKs are like every other kid and mishandle their relationship with their child. A PK needs to know that they are loved by their parents, and that in their life you are their parent first then the Pastor, First Lady, or whatever your title may be. The expectations and pressures placed on these kids are sometimes too high, and when they don't meet our expectation, we pour on the guilt. As a mom to two PKs, I was guilty of this.

For some PKs, the pressure and guilt we pour out can impact them for years, causing them to carry their own form of secret guilt, and unless they share it with us or God reveals it, we may never even know it's there, so it's important to ask God to reveal to you anything that your kids may be harboring or struggling with based on the pressures and guilt you may have placed on them. I'm reminded of an event involving our son, Napolian.

One night, he was meeting us at the restaurant for dinner. As he sat down, I noticed that his ears were pierced. Now, if you know the C.O.G.I.C. (Church of God in Christ) way, then you also know that's a big NO! So, I looked at him with my religious and sanctified self and said, "I'm so disappointed in you. Why would you get your ears pierced?" When I said this to him, I was only thinking and speaking from a judgmental place. I was much more concerned about what my church would say or think, and how this would reflect on me as a mom. When you're harboring secret guilt, you tend to view everything through the lens of "What if they find out?!" even if it has nothing to do with the issue you're hiding.

But my son looked at me with tears in his eyes and said, "Mom! That's how you feel about your son who's about to graduate with honors, never been in trouble in school, faithful to ministry, always supporting you guys – my parents – and Mom, that's all you can say?" He got up to leave, and I was so hurt from seeing the hurt in his eyes. I realized quickly that I was wrong, and as my son expressed his hurts, I had to make this right. I had to figure out a way to administer healing to this wound, which I inflicted on him as his mom because he didn't meet my expectations. He needed to be healed and shown love as a son. He also needed to see his mom humble herself, acknowledge her wrong, and ask for forgiveness.

I tore down my pride and religious strongholds, and I freed my son to know that he was accepted and loved, and that he was free to be himself and express himself in the way that he had chosen without condemnation from me. If I hadn't, this situation could've have given Satan room in his life, and room to wreck our relationship. Every time my son looked in the mirror, or received a compliment about his earrings, he would have been reminded of guilt, either the guilt that he didn't live up to his mother's expectations, or the actual guilt that I tried to dish upon him. Either way, I wasn't letting guilt move into his house.

Before my son left that restaurant that day, I allowed God in me and my love for my son to move me to take the next steps and fix the situation. We must love and pray for our children, but we must also admit when we have wronged them and fix the situation. Like all kids, PKs have to see us walk in love and humility if we're going to maintain a solid relationship with them, and if they're truly going to walk out their calling and God-given identity.

We want our kids to love God, but they also have to learn how to love themselves and be who God has called them to be. As with any kid, PKs might not have the same gifts and ministries as their parents, but they do have their own gifts and their own ministry, so if they're going to live unaffected by guilt, be intentional about allowing them to find out who God has designed them to be. When Napolian was growing up, our late Pastor, Bishop W.S. Harris said to my husband and I, "Whatever y'all do, allow him to be a kid. Don't take his identity away from him." He went on to say "So many parents of PKs rob the kids of their childhood." That helped us a lot.

The best thing you can do for your child is to understand that they are God's child first. As a parent, you are just stewards over them. As parents, it's ok for us to have expectations, desires, and goals for our children, but we have to be careful about what we are communicating when they don't measure up to what we expect or desire, and we have to be careful that our pride doesn't flare up. I believe we as parents need to communicate to our children that what they do is important to us. It's important to let them know that what they do matters to us and it matters to God. It's important to acknowledge your children's strengths and also help them recognize and improve upon their weaknesses.

They should be held to great standards, but they should also have room to grow. They should know that you expect them to error at some point in life, and that we don't expect them to be perfect. Mistakes and wrong decisions are a part of growing up. Let them know that you expect for them to win, but also to lose sometimes, they will have good days and bad days, but they don't have to fear because God will be with them. Teach them Psalm 56:3 *"When I am afraid, I will trust in you."* This will give them something to stand on when the hard times come, even if those hard times come while living under your roof.

Let them know that God calls them blessed. Remind them that God will be with them through it all – the good decisions and the bad ones. Be intentional about encouraging them to open up and share their feelings. Set an atmosphere for them to be able to do that. Let them know that you expect for them to win but also to lose sometimes, and whether they win or whether they lose, it doesn't matter. What does matter is that they aim high and do their best. And if they fall, you expect them not to stay down, but to get up; to arise. They should know that you expect them to get up and bounce back from any fall, and that God's hand is waiting for them to reach up and give him theirs. If you are intentional about instilling these principles in your children, even if you've already messed up, it will help you build a strong relationship and protect you from falling victim to pride when they make the wrong choice. These are the principles that my husband and I eventually learned to do with our children, and it works.

Pride is a problem when a mother or father is more concerned about their titles --- whether you're in ministry and carry the title of Pastor, Teacher, Preacher, Evangelist, First Lady, etc. or whether you're in a high profile position in business or your local community -- than your child. It's a problem when you can't feel your child's pain, or you choose to see it and overlook it because they've disappointed you. I can't express it enough. Even when you feel they have let you down, tell them that they're going to be ok, and remind them that God is still for them, in spite of what you feel or what they've done. Don't let pride make you become so self-centered that you lose or damage your relationship with your child.

Pride will cause you to do more damage to that child, that teen-mom, or son who might have an addiction or be living a lifestyle that is different from your beliefs, like the child who is dealing with homosexuality or anything that goes against your beliefs or culture. Pride has ruined many relationships. Stop worrying about you and your feelings and take on the heart of Christ when it gets hard for you to accept or deal with your child. In Jeremiah 30:17, it is written, "I will restore you to health and heal your wounds declares the Lord." God is offering hope to every person and every situation, and we should do the same rather than issuing guilt.

I can say today that our children and I have a strong bond and a close friendship, but that only came with work, humility, love, lots of patience, and much prayer. If you're struggling with this as a parent, ask God to help you understand your child, but most of all be willing to admit when you're wrong, and have much patience. Let them be who God has called them to be. Speak into their lives, forgive them, and love them when it seems impossible. Even when they make mistakes or choose the wrong road, they still need your love. Pray for them and love them through whatever season or phase they're going through. Our children need to know that if they come to a crossroad in their lives that they have parents that will hold their hands and walk through their valleys and pray them through it. The devil desires to have your children, so you must oppose the enemy and fight for them. Don't allow pride or guilt to ruin your relationship with your children.

One of the most important things that you can do is to give your children back to God and ask him to shield them and keep them. Sometimes they will need to be shielded from the enemy's tactics. Sometimes it will be from the decisions they make. They may need to be shielded from the company they keep (which you should always pay attention to), or what they may need to be shielded from until you are completely whole, may be you. Either way, God is so faithful, and he will do it. If you feel like you're failing as a parent, ask him to help you. I'm a living witness, he will.

Children are a blessing and a gift from the Lord.

Psalm 127:3

TIPS FOR PARENTS

Being a parent can be tough. Here are some lessons that I've learned over the years that hopefully will help you as well:

- o Focus on becoming a good listener

- o Make quality time for them and pray with them

- o Let them know that they're valued and loved

- o Speak life over them and into them

- o Speak faith confessions over them

- o Be quick to apologize when you're wrong

Confessions:

- o My children are hungry for God. (Eph 1:17-18).

- o I declare that my children love God and are sensitive to this voice. They are hungry for the things of the Spirit.

- o Revelation from God flows to them. They see and understand spiritual things.

- o They know what God has called them to do, and they want to do it.

- o My children are overcomers. (1 John 4:4, Romans 8:37)

o The Greater One is in my children. He helps them, guides them, encourages them, protects them, and empowers them today. He is greater than any plan or force of the enemy.

CHAPTER FOURTEEN

Protecting Your Daughter from a Lifetime of Guilt

Friend, if your daughter is pregnant and thinking about having an abortion, I encourage you to think twice about it. I wish someone would have told me what to expect after having an abortion. It's not a quick solution no matter what they tell you at the clinic. What she's about to do will turn into years of regrets, guilt, and shame, and she can't undo it once it is done.

Abortion seems like such an easy fix, but it's not. They'll tell you it's a quick procedure, and to expect some cramps and light vaginal bleeding. They may even tell you that it feels like strong period cramps, and how they can give you medication to make it hurt less and numb the pain. They may even assure you that they'll try to make you as comfortable as possible, and then you can go home to rest. But what they won't tell you is that the minute you have the abortion, there is something else unleashed in your life that causes a different type of pain. It's a pain that only God himself can fix.

When you go through with having an abortion, it's like signing a contract that locks you in, and makes you the responsible party held accountable to this debt. If you're a mom and your daughter is considering having an abortion, tell her that you will stand with her in her decision to have her child and love her through the process. Give her the confidence that she and her baby will be loved and supported. Remind her that God loves her and is willing to help her. She needs to trust him through the process and invite him into the situation. Stress to her that if she chooses to have an abortion, she's going to carry a deep dark secret and she's signing up to carry secret guilt that will change her and affect her emotions terribly. It opens the door for Satan to torment her with accusations and lies, because he is the father of lies.

Unfortunately, this is not just my experience. I wish I could say that I was the only one who went through this and had this negative experience. But as you come across the brave women who've had abortions and are healed enough to speak about it publicly, you'll find this is the experience for most women.

Don't fall for the lie, my friend. An abortion will not fix the problem. Encourage her to lean on God for his strength to get through the pregnancy, the judgmental actions and opinions of others (and there will be) but think beyond your feelings.

The effects of having an abortion will be more damaging than you can imagine, and it's not worth it. The pain is so real. A lot of pain and many problems in her life after the abortion will be from the root of the abortion regarding the baby's life that was stolen or taken in the procedure. No one explained this to me. Encourage her to embrace her pregnancy.

Before you make such a decision about taking her to have an abortion, do these things first:

- Pray with her and for her

- Remind her that God has a plan for her life even in the mess-up, and that it's not the end of the world.

- If you're having a hard time with the idea of encouraging her not to have an abortion, pray and ask God to help you submit your will to his, and to help you see this situation through his eyes. Tell him how you feel about this situation and ask him to show you what to do. "Not my will, Lord, but your will be done." Make this a part of your prayer. He knows exactly how to make his will known when invited into the conversation.

- Make sure she has enough information to truly

make an informed decision. This should include:

• An unbiased discussion about the options available to her for an unplanned pregnancy -- abortion, adoption, raising the child

• more information about the process from a medical perspective. Before she can have an abortion, she'll need an abortion assessment.

• Where she can find support services and resources if you don't have the money to support her.

During an abortion assessment, you may:

• Discuss your reasons for considering an abortion and make sure you're sure about your decision.

• Be offered the chance to talk things over with a trained counselor if you think it might help

• Talk to a nurse or doctor about the abortion methods available, including any associated risks and complications

• Be offered an ultrasound scan to check how many weeks pregnant you are

• Be offered testing for sexually transmitted infections (STDs)

• Need to have other tests such as blood tests (depending on any medical conditions you have or the stage you're at in the pregnancy).

• Just as you would with making an informed decision about any major decision, medical, financial or otherwise, you should encourage her to get opinions about other people's experiences with having an abortion. Now, I realize that most abortions are done in secrecy, and this is not something that she may feel comfortable asking people about. If this is the case, you may want to get her books written by people who have been where she is and chose abortion as the best route for them. *Journey of Healing: Finding Hope and Healing After an Abortion, by Myrtzie Levell,* is a great read. It's a collection of personal stories by 12 different women.

• Reach out for support as you go through this process. This is one of the things we do at Brenda Barnes Ministries.

You can reach us at **www.BrendaBarnes.org**

CHAPTER FIFTEEN

For My Sisters

I pray as you went on this journey with me, you are now on your way to healing and being set free from all guilt and shame. Although I have a passion for people who are living in bondage to guilt, my true passion is for women who know what it's like to deal with the secret guilt and emotional pain of an abortion. If that's you, I'm writing this chapter specifically for you. If that's not you, thank you for going on this journey with me and listening to my story. You may want to skip ahead. To my sister who has had an abortion, this is for you.

If you're like many of us, you hide the guilt of an abortion very deep in your heart. You already know abortions can be one of the most traumatic experiences you and I have ever gone through in life. When you are post-abortive, you learn to live in silence and secrecy and bury hurts deep inside, which causes you to struggle with repressed memories of guilt, shame, anger, depression, and so much more. This was the place that I dwelled for years, and I learned that the more you hold on to these negative emotions, this burden that you carry keeps you feeling like a failure and afraid to reveal your hidden pain. You find yourself isolated.

You've already read my story so I won't go over the details again, but I can't tell you how many times I can recall easing into another room, feeling completely overtaken with emotion from where I was reliving memories of the day I aborted my baby. I looked for every opportunity to weep over the thought of what I'd done, not realizing just how broken and bruised I was. I was always beating myself up over it; wondering how I could have done what I did, whether it was a boy or girl, or how old it would have been, and apologizing to God for not giving it a chance to live. Then there would the inner conversations I'd have with my baby, telling it I was sorry. Abortions come with attachments that you live with until you are ready to be totally free of the deep pain that is the aftermath of an abortion.

I pray that my transparency brings healing to you, with God's help and his love leading the way on this journey. I'm not saying that it will always be easy, but I am saying that when you ask God to help you and heal every area, I promise you he will. He did it for me, and he is the same God who loves you so much, and cares for you as well. Just trust him. He's not angry with you. He hasn't condemned you -- in spite of what people who represent him on Earth, may have the tendency to make you feel, when you hear them speak of abortion. Forgiveness, healing, and a fresh start is available to you and anyone who asks. It is my prayer that God will use this book as a tool to help guide you to your place of healing. You are not alone, and you didn't come across this book by chance. He wants you to be healed and restored and is ready to show his power and glory in your life. Jeremiah 30:17 says, *"For I will restore health unto thee, and I will heal thee of thy wounds, saith the Lord."*

I want to encourage you. Do whatever it takes to make sure you are healed and the bleeding stops, so that God can reveal to you the people you were sent to heal and he can bring a new sense of fulfillment and freedom into your life like you've never experienced before. It's worth the fight to get free. I shared with you some of the struggles I had with getting back in God's presence after the abortion. From where my mom left this strong legacy of prayer for me and my sisters, I never forgot how to talk to God and drop things at his feet, but I had stopped talking with him in a way that would birth my healing. Mostly, I was just apologizing all the time. I had to fight my way in his presence because of the pain that was so great. Sometimes I couldn't pray. All I could do is cry.

I would put my worship songs on and weep in his presence. I also understood later, that when I got up from prayer, I wasn't leaving the hurt there. I was taking it back, causing my healing to be delayed. As you begin this journey, make sure you're leaving things at his feet. You've suffered this long, don't delay your healing. Show up to get in his presence even if you don't think he's listening. Even if you don't feel like it. Be consistent in saying your declarations. Treat it as if your life depends upon it, because it does. Your future, your ministry, and the life that God has for you can't work effectively until you get healed.

I remember having the desire to be used by God. I had this yearning to heal other ladies and I thought I was ready. One evening I called this pastor, Dr. Yvonne Capehart. I remember the pain that I felt sharing my story with her telling her how I had a mandate on my life to heal hurting women and that I was ready to minister to anyone who had dealt with the pain of guilt and shame after an abortion. While I was sharing my experience with her, I couldn't finish talking about my abortion and how I killed my baby without crying.

The pain got stronger. I started feeling like it had just happened all over again. I shared with her that these women needed to be healed if they've suffered from abortions like me. While I was talking, I hadn't even noticed that I couldn't get through my story without crying. She listened to me patiently. When I was done, her words to me were: "Evangelist Brenda, you need to be healed first before you can offer healing to these women that God intends for you to heal."

She went on to say, "Let God heal you." I remember hanging up the phone, feeling what I like to call "some kind of way" (that's when you're feeling something that's not good, but you're not sure exactly WHICH emotion you're feeling, if not several at one time). I was left wondering if she fully heard my heart.

After hanging up the phone I went before the Lord in prayer. I cried out to him, "Lord, heal me of this pain! Please take it away. I want you to use this pain for your purpose," I said. I began to just praise him in my place of pain. I praised him over my pain, until I found myself in a state where I was just talking to him and thanking him. I remember feeling the pain leaving me. I was reminded that day of the truth that in his presence was the place I could go to sort through my feelings and release my hurt, anger, guilt, and shame. It was in the quiet place that brought me in his presence.

I later realized that there were more benefits waiting for me by being in the presence of God. Healing, joy, peace, calmness, and forgiveness to name a few. When you spend time with him, guilt and shame is removed, anger has to go, and depression has to go because you are in his presence. You must welcome his presence and take whatever steps necessary to make sure you get in it. You can start by playing soft worship music. Play something that lifts up his name, and not your problem and not your pain. Don't worry about what you're going to say. Just talk to him like you're talking to someone. Later, read a scripture and next start just glorifying him and magnifying him with whatever words, and in whatever ways you know how, or feel connected to him in doing. Some people sing. Some dance. Some write poetry. Some just talk. There's no best way. It's personal between you and him. These are just some of the ways to get in his presence. You are in his presence now; he hears you.

Thou wilt make known of me the path of life; In Thy presence is fulness of joy; In Thy right hand there are pleasures forever. You will gain strength in the presence of the lord.

Psalm 16:11

The Joy of The Lord Is My Strength.

Nehemiah 8:10

Nehemiah 8:10 was one my Mother's favorite Bible verses. The Joy of The Lord is my strength, when you have no Joy, you have no Strength. When we experience joy, it will allow you to attract more joyful people. That's why it's important to get in God's presence. Choose to dwell in the lord's presence, don't dwell in your guilt and shame. This was a process, but I got it. It took me years to get to this place. I'm so glad that I got healed first, before trying to minister healing to other women. If I hadn't, my pain and anger could have bled on them, and I could have wounded them thinking that I was bringing healing.

The truth is hurting people hurt people.

I'm yet thanking God for Dr. Capehart for sharing the light on my needing to be healed. As the years went by, I knew I was healed, and am now able to share my story with anyone. First to my daughter, which marked the beginning of chains being broken off me and any young ladies that came across my path who were dealing with guilt of abuse or an abortion. I began to speak to hundreds of women. As I'd share my story, I'd watch the altars fill with women coming for prayers to be set free from the guilt and shame of abortion or abuse. There would often be a pastor's wife – one who was in my position where she was ministering to others and carrying her own secret, who'd open up about her experience and begin her journey of getting free from the guilt, after I'd minister at an event and share my story. Why am I sharing this with you?

To make this point: We don't overcome pain and struggle and hard times just for ourselves. Our pain becomes our purpose. When we get healed and free, we can heal and set others free! We must make sure we use our pain to minister healing and wholeness to others! Don't let them suffer alone while you are holding on to your image at the expense of their freedom. Make sure you're healed so you don't bleed on others. You've made it this far. Lean wholly on the Lord, and continue your journey of healing, whether it's through finding a Christian counselor who specializes in this, finding someone who will pray with you or a support group.

If you don't have access to support or don't know anyone who can help, you're welcome to join me in my online community with other women who have gone through similar situations or join us on one of our national prayer calls. You can find out more information at www.BrendaBarnes.org. If you are looking for therapy or counseling, I am not a therapist or psychologist, but I can point you in the right direction. The following associations have Christian Counselors, which may be a good start for you.

The National Association of Christian Counselors:

https://nacconline.org/find-a-counselor/

American Association of Christian Counselors:

https://www.aacc.net/

Final Thoughts:

Thank you for allowing me to share my story with you and going on this journey with me. Hopefully this has helped you farther along your journey. Before we part, I'd like to pray this over your life.

Lord Jesus, I pray for every person who deals with some form of secret guilt and shame. Lord heal them of all silent guilt and pain. Free them of all the residue from guilt and help them see you as their father and healer. Lord, uproot all hidden pain and their deep dark secrets. Help them to understand that your grace is sufficient, and that your mercy is new every morning.

Lord, help them to know that they are forgiven of every sin when they ask. For the teen who cries herself to sleep at night thinking she's the only one who has made a bad choice, Father God, touch her. Let our daughters and sons feel your love. Remind them they are not alone and that they are loved and cared for. Allow them to experience your hope and peace. Help them to seek the right guidance and make the right choices that won't come back and haunt them. Lord break every chain of bondage off their minds. Lord, let them know they can cast all of their cares on you Jesus for you care for them.

I ask that you put your loving arms around them, restore their joy and help them to forgive themselves of every burden. Lord, touch every mother and every father. Give them the love and wisdom to stand with their child or children through every challenge. Give them strength and be the glue to hold them together. In Jesus' name we pray. Amen.

Want to stay connected?

Join the online community @

BrendaBarnes.org/Free2Soar

About the Author

Author, Inspirational Speaker, and Psalmist, Brenda Barnes is the Founder of Brenda Barnes Ministries. Driven by a passion to inspire and equip women who have experienced the trauma of abortion or abuse,  she has been a beacon of light for hundreds of women, as both a speaker and former Co-Pastor of Victory Temple Church, which she and her husband, Napolian Barnes, Sr. founded and pastored for 18 years.

As a survivor who has personally experienced the same trauma as the women she serves, Brenda brings a practical and relevant message of hope and healing of emotional wounds and a message of freedom from guilt and shame to women everywhere. Annually, she hosts a Survivor's Conference where hundreds of women are healed and set free from domestic violence and Cancer survivors are celebrated. From workshops to keynote events, her transparent and authentic message, combined with a powerful gift of Intercessory Prayer, has made her a draw for women's ministries, women's shelters, churches, and organizations that help young women choose life. As the founder of Family Menders, Brenda is an advocate for family restoration, as well as a resource for Single Moms who decide to choose life and keep their babies. Through her project, Moms Wee Care, her ministry comes alongside young women to provide baby items and other essentials. She is also a Mentor and Counselor for Wiregrass Hope Center in Southeast Alabama.

Married to her husband of 39+ years, Napolian Barnes, Sr., Brenda resides in Dothan, Alabama and is the mother to two adult children, Napolian Barnes, Jr. and Precious Barnes Abbott, and is Gamma to 2 beautiful grandchildren and counting. For more information or to invite Brenda to your event, visit:

www.BrendaBarnes.org.

Made in the USA
Columbia, SC
23 September 2024